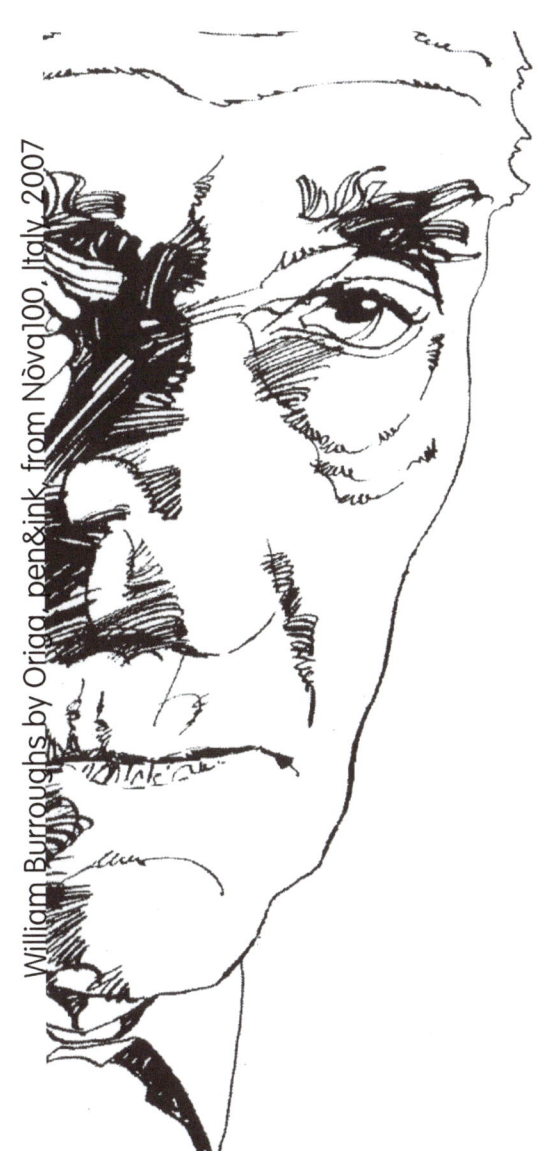

William Burroughs by Origa pen&ink from Nòva100, Italy 2007

FACES

Portraits by Graziano Origa

FACES
Published by Rossi Projects LLC
New York - New York 2009

Author Graziano Origa
Graphic Design Daniel Rossi
Copyright Origa Foundation Italy 2009
ISBN 978-0-578-01847-8

www.origa-punkartist.mayancaper.net
www.grazianooriga.nova100.ilsole24ore.com
www.origafoundation.wordpress.com

www.rossiprojects.com

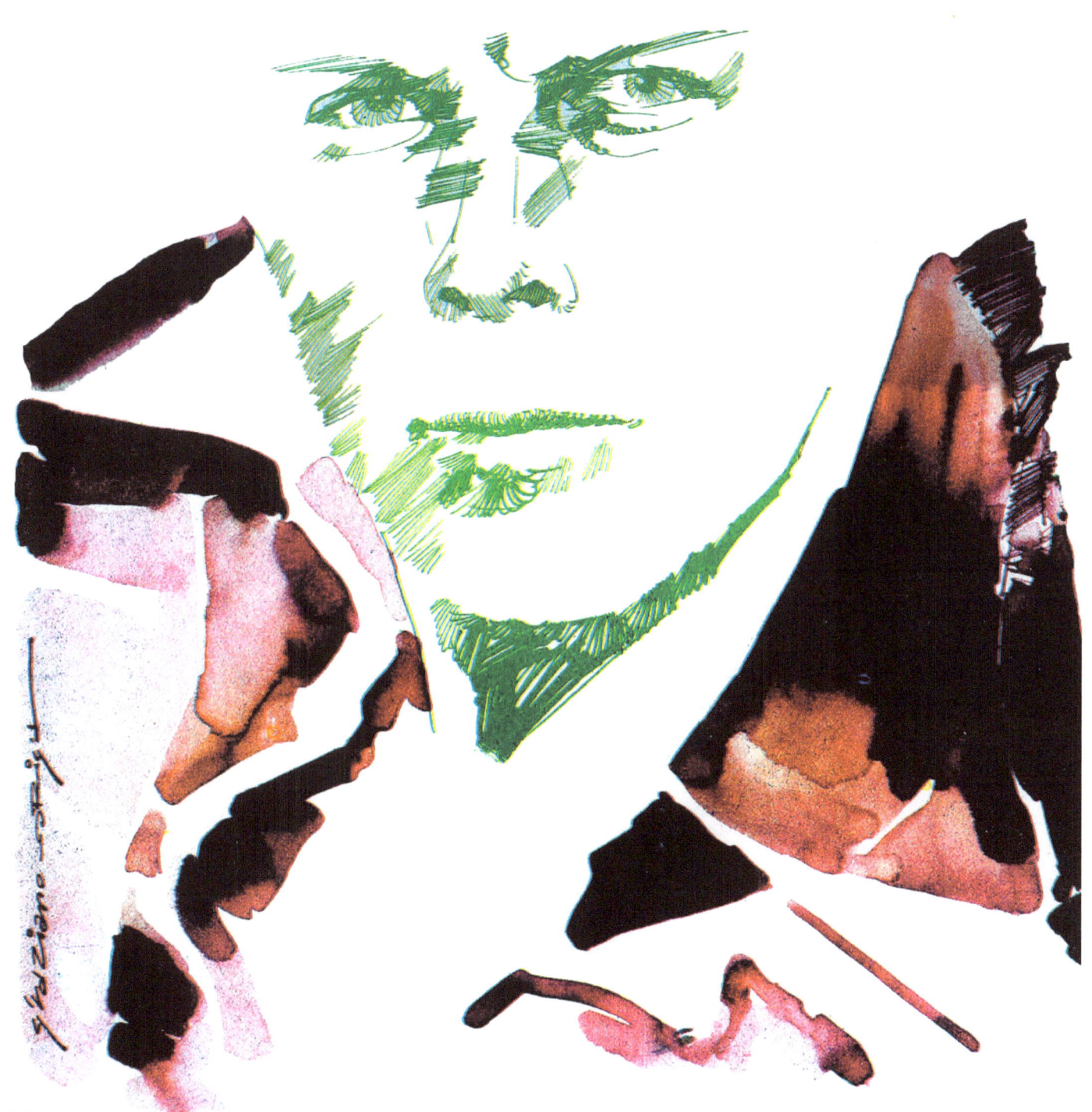

(3) Giorgio Armani

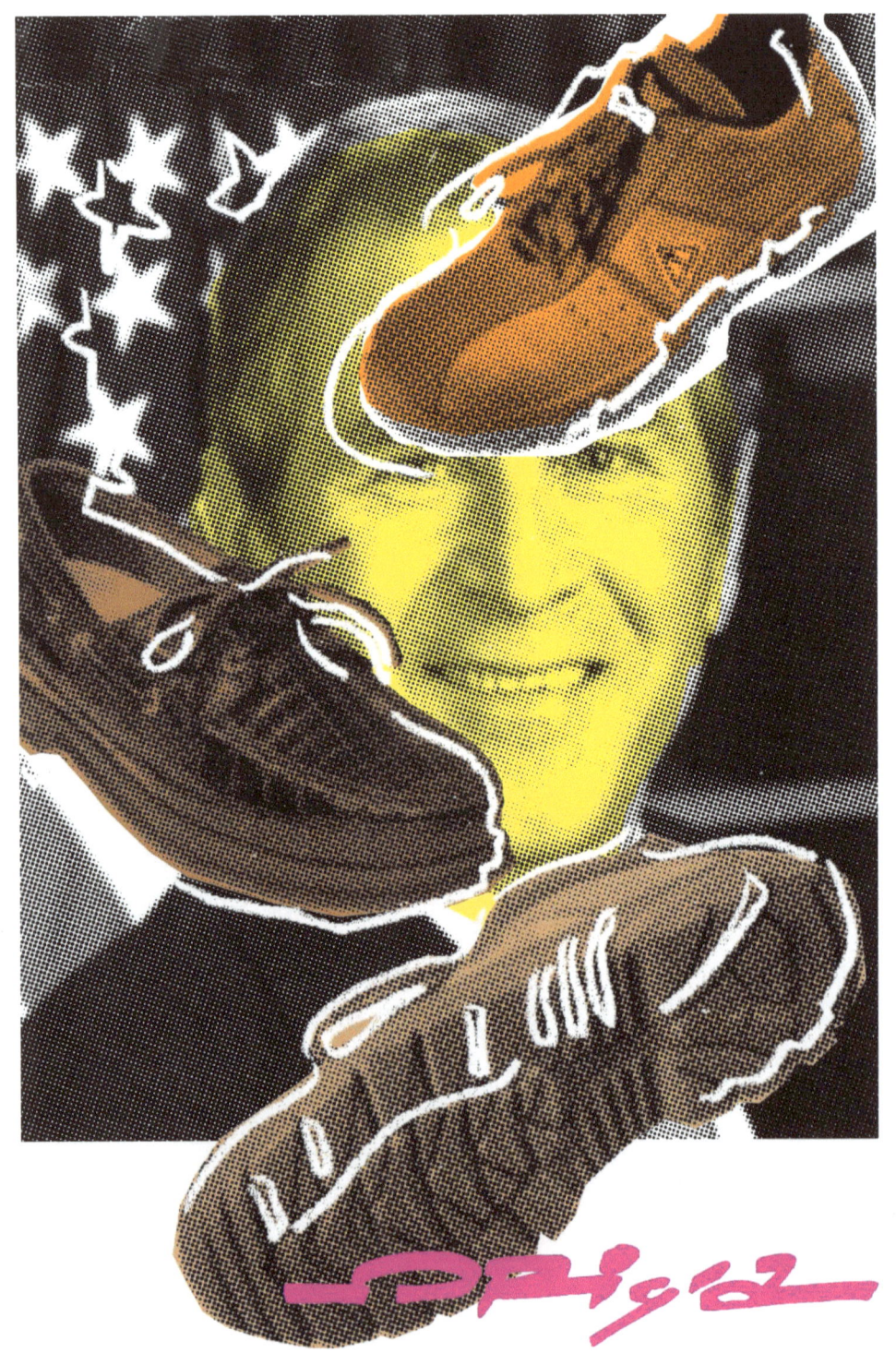

(4) George Bush

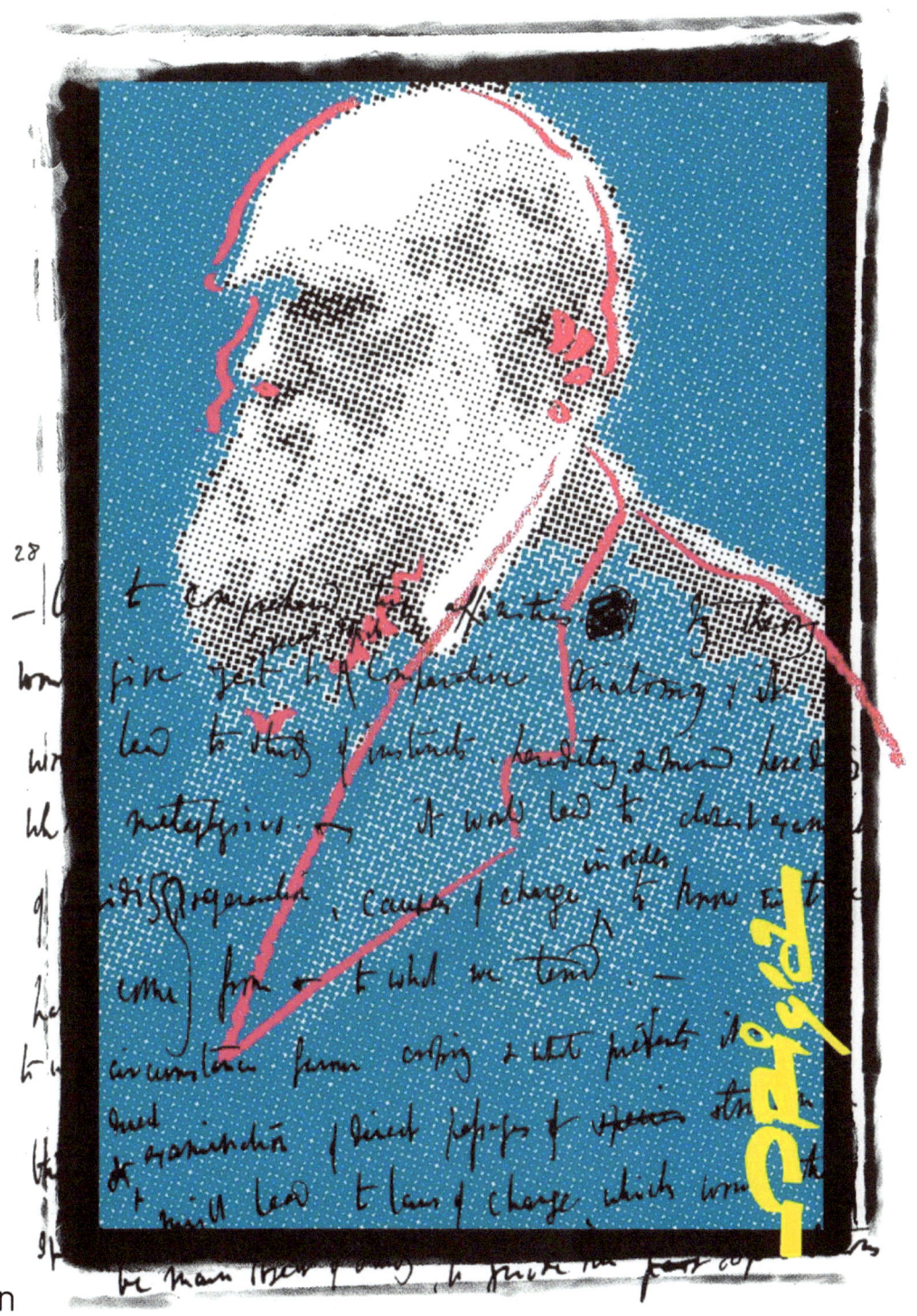

(5) Charles Robert Darwin

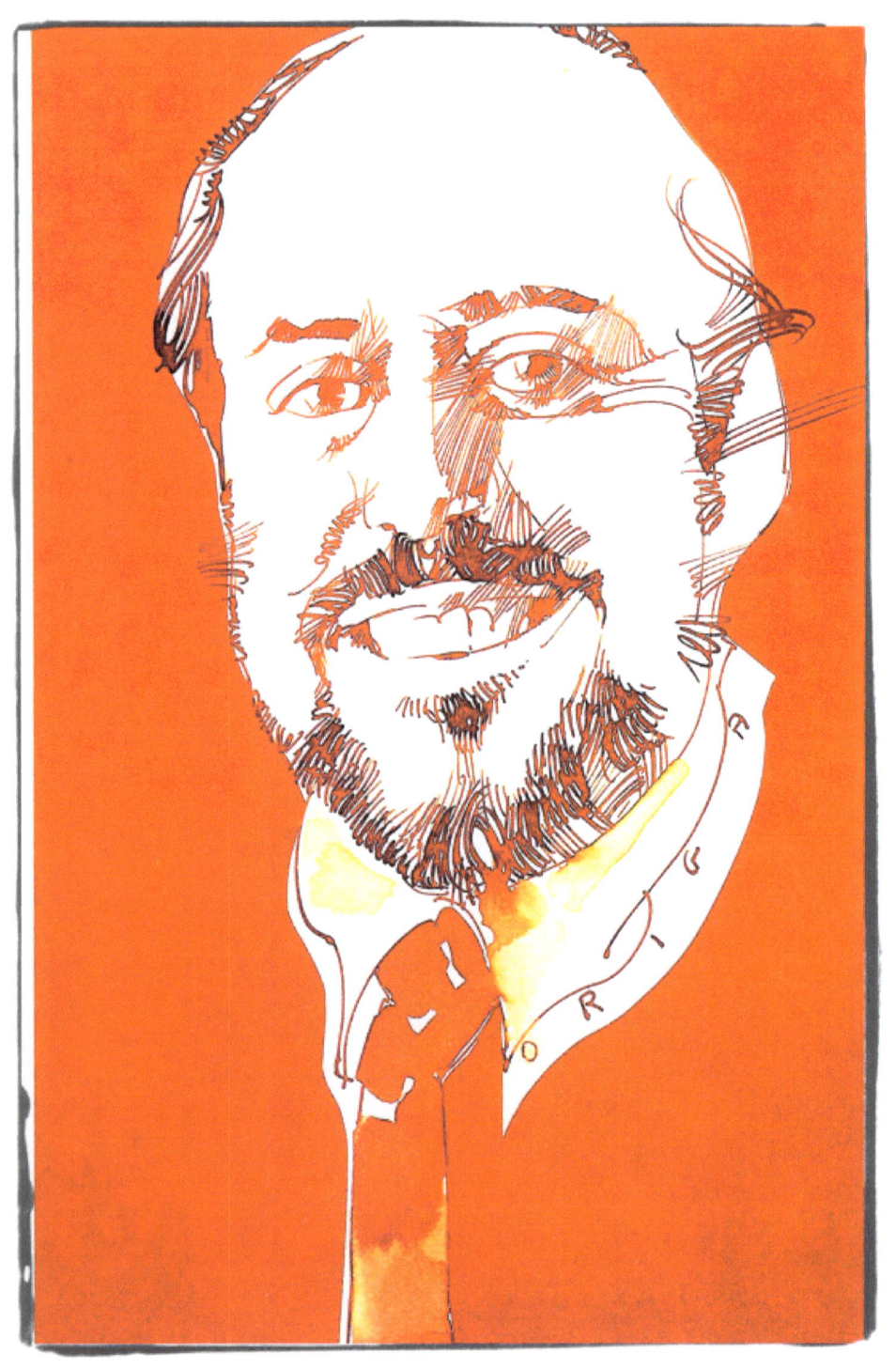

(6) Elio Fiorucci

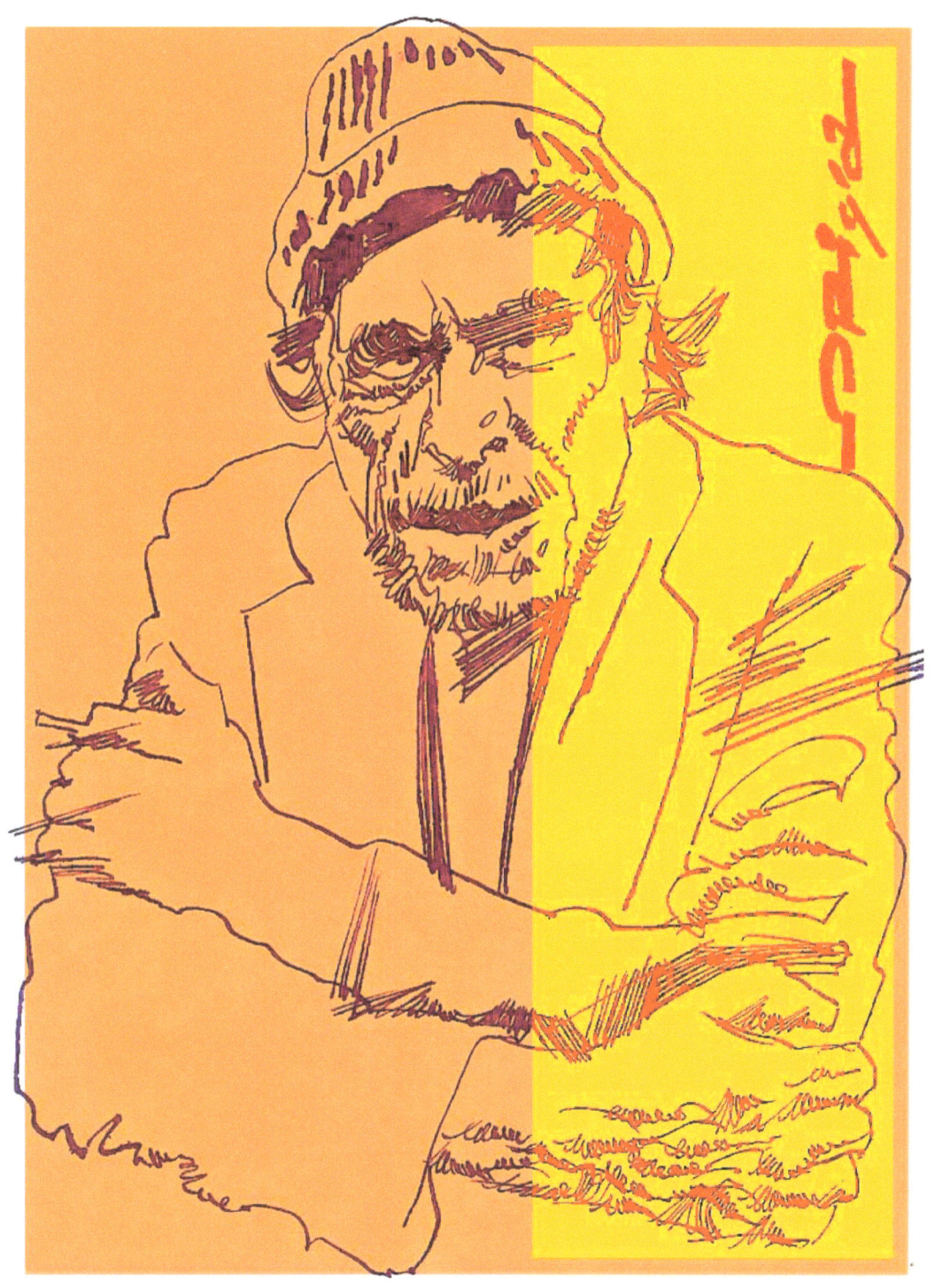

(7) Charles Bukowski

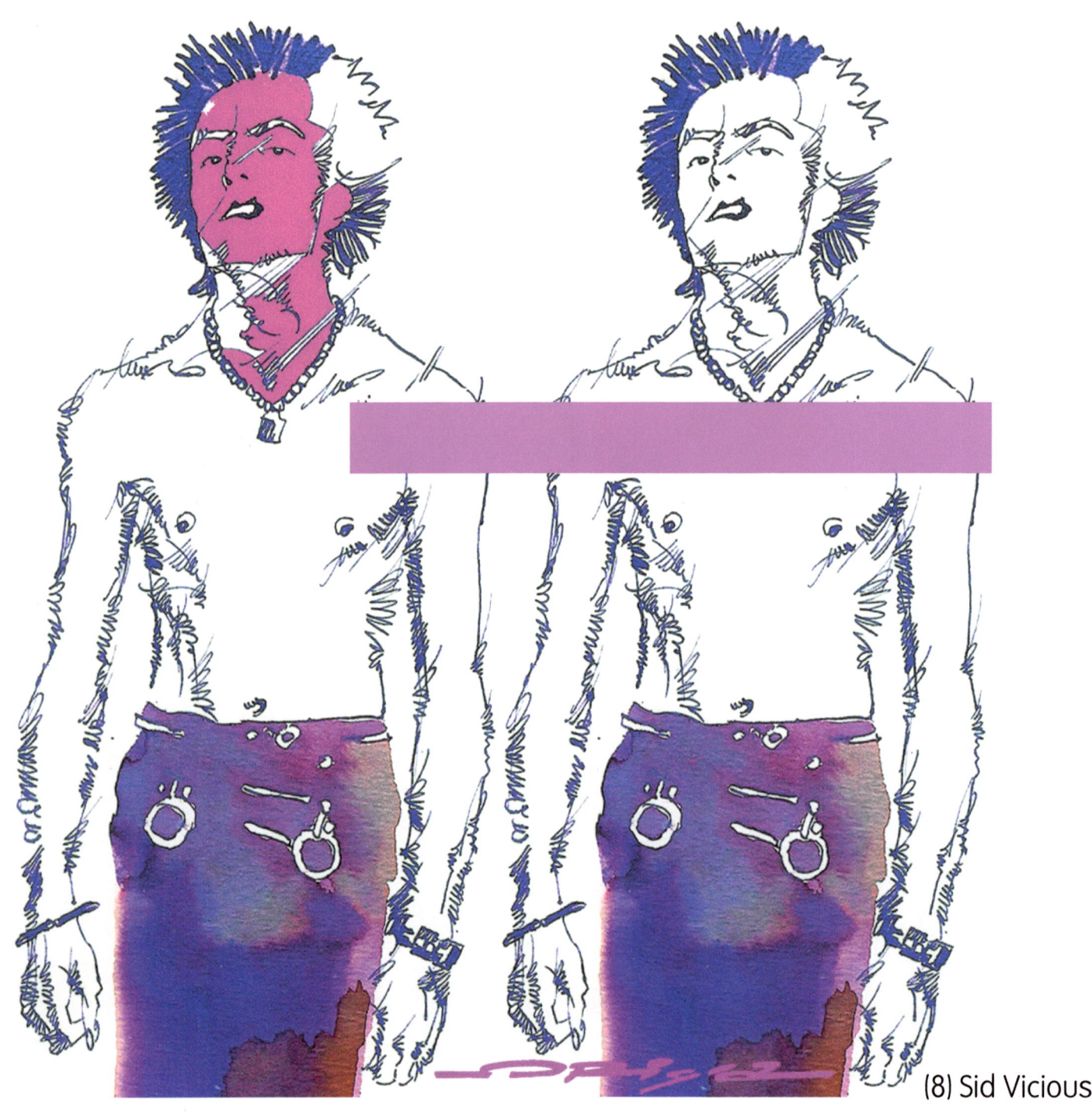

(8) Sid Vicious

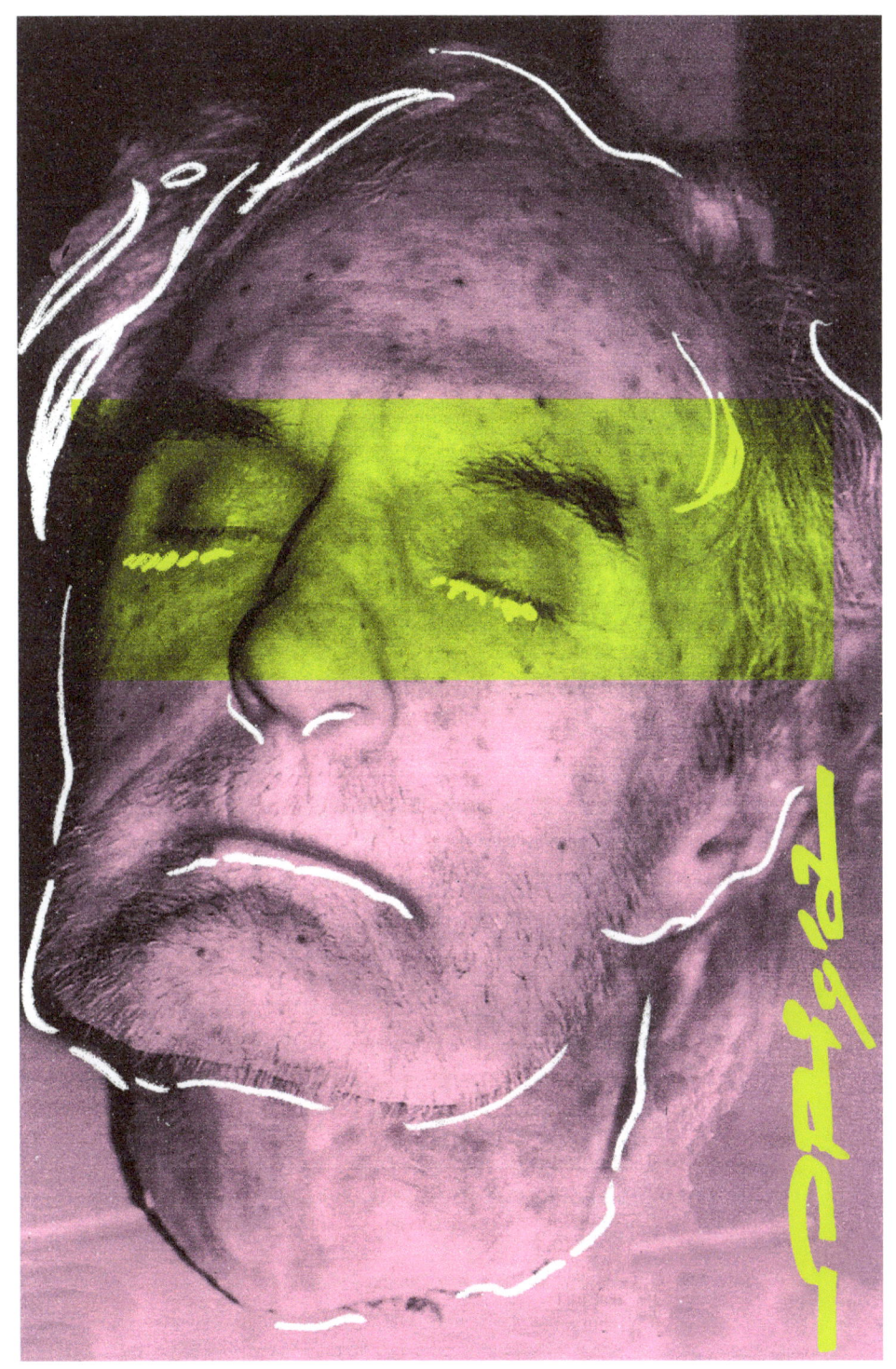

(9) Timothy Leary

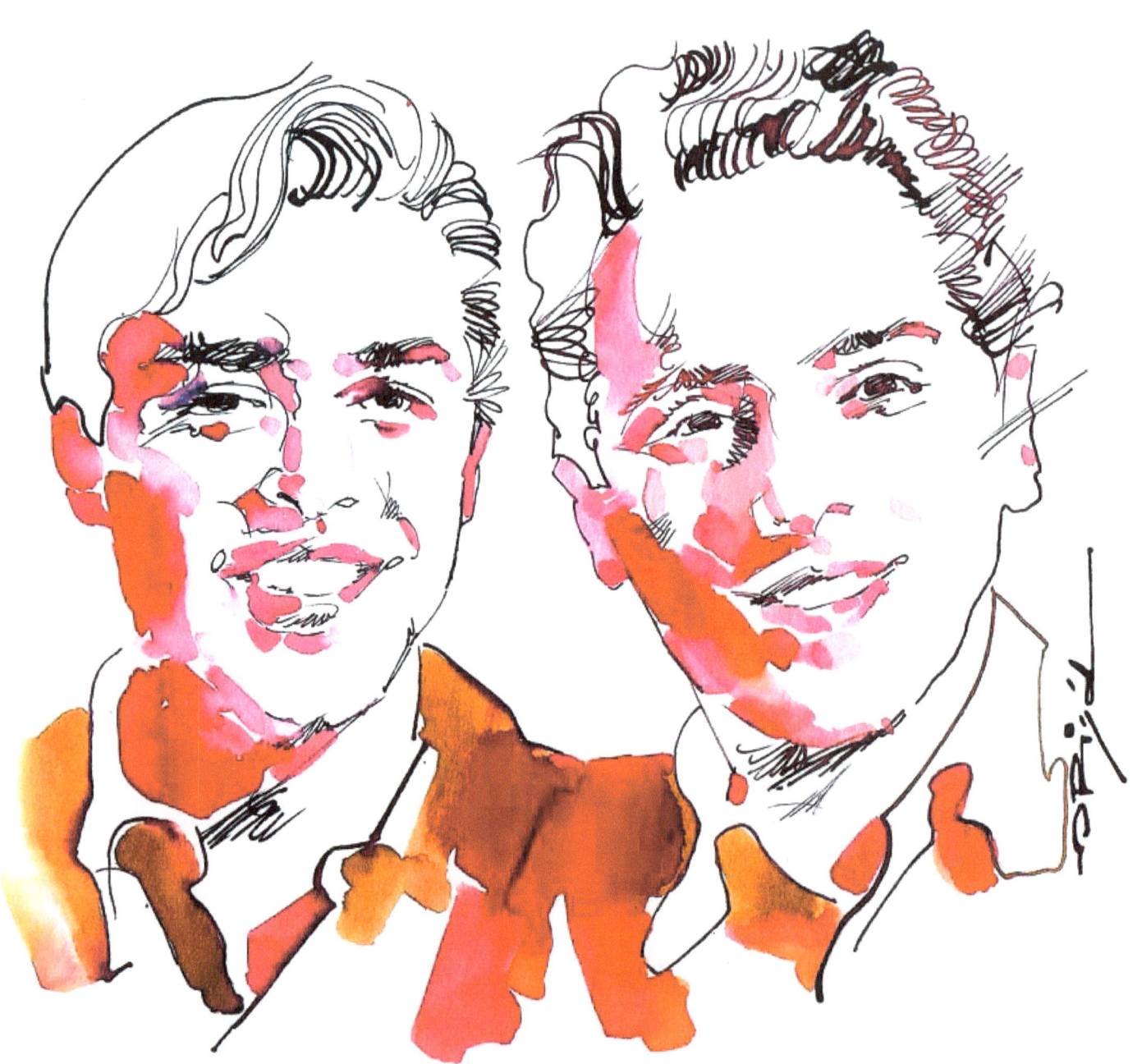

(10) Sergey Brin & Larry Page

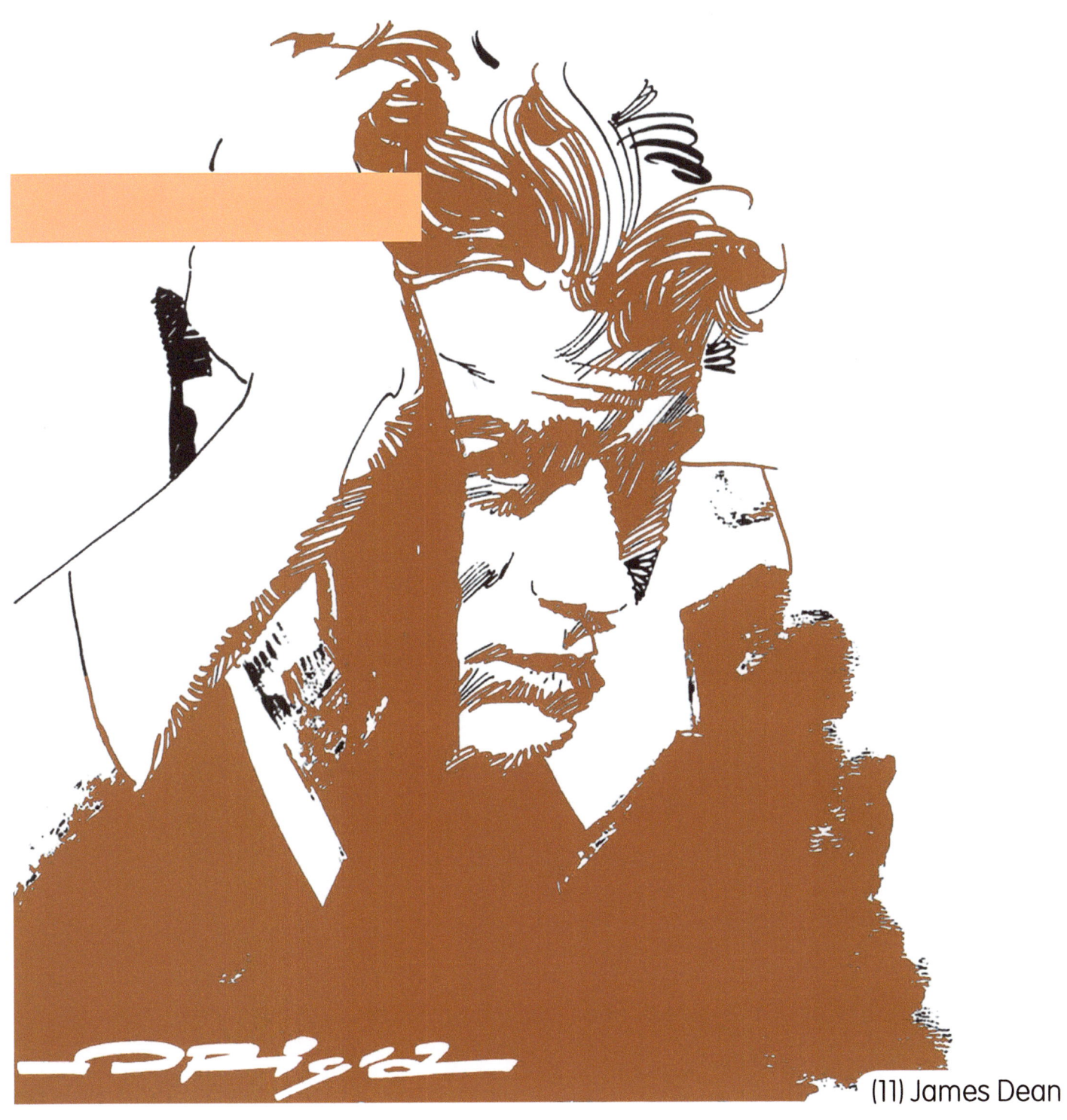

(11) James Dean

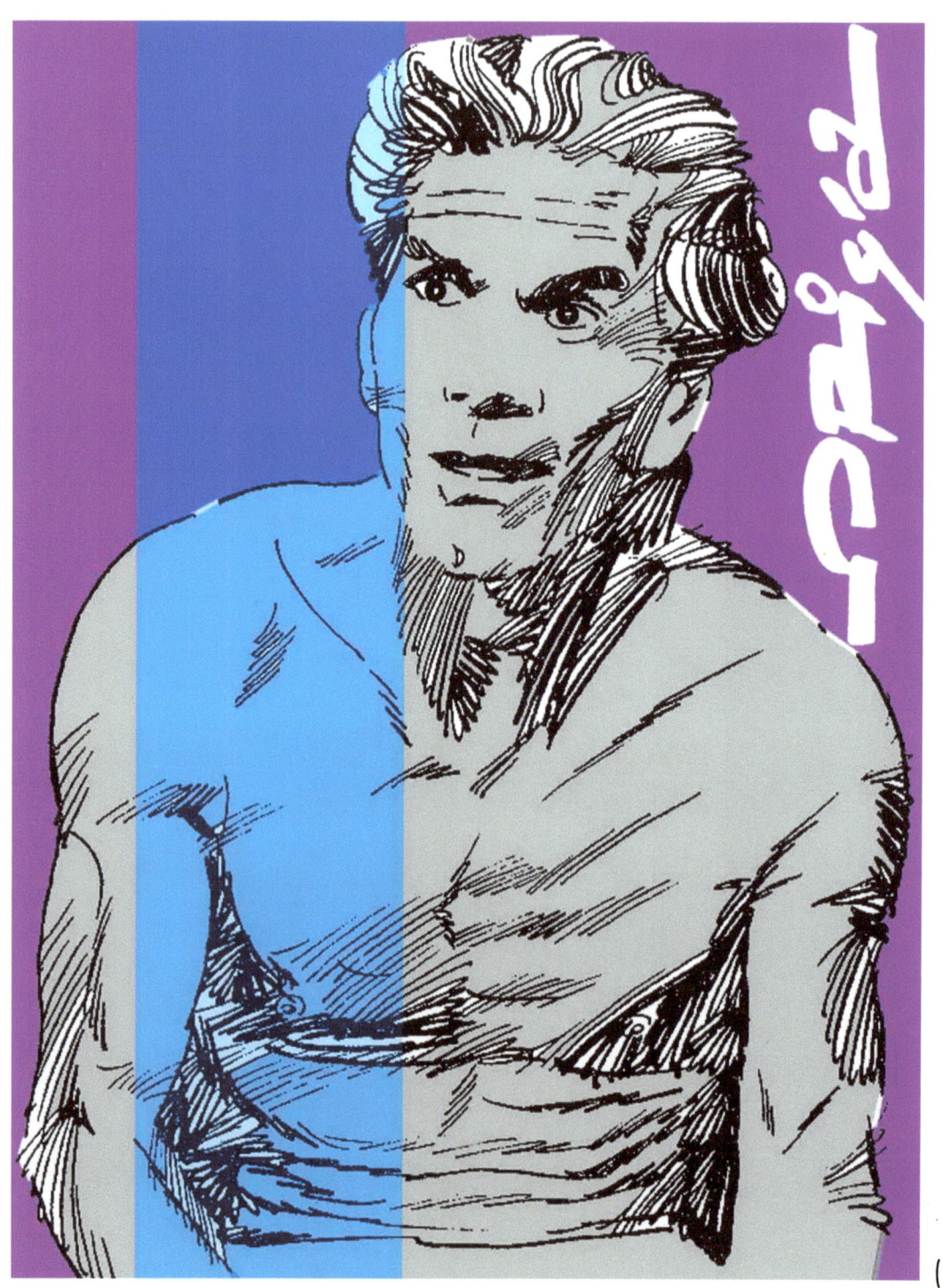

(12) Pier Paolo Pasolini

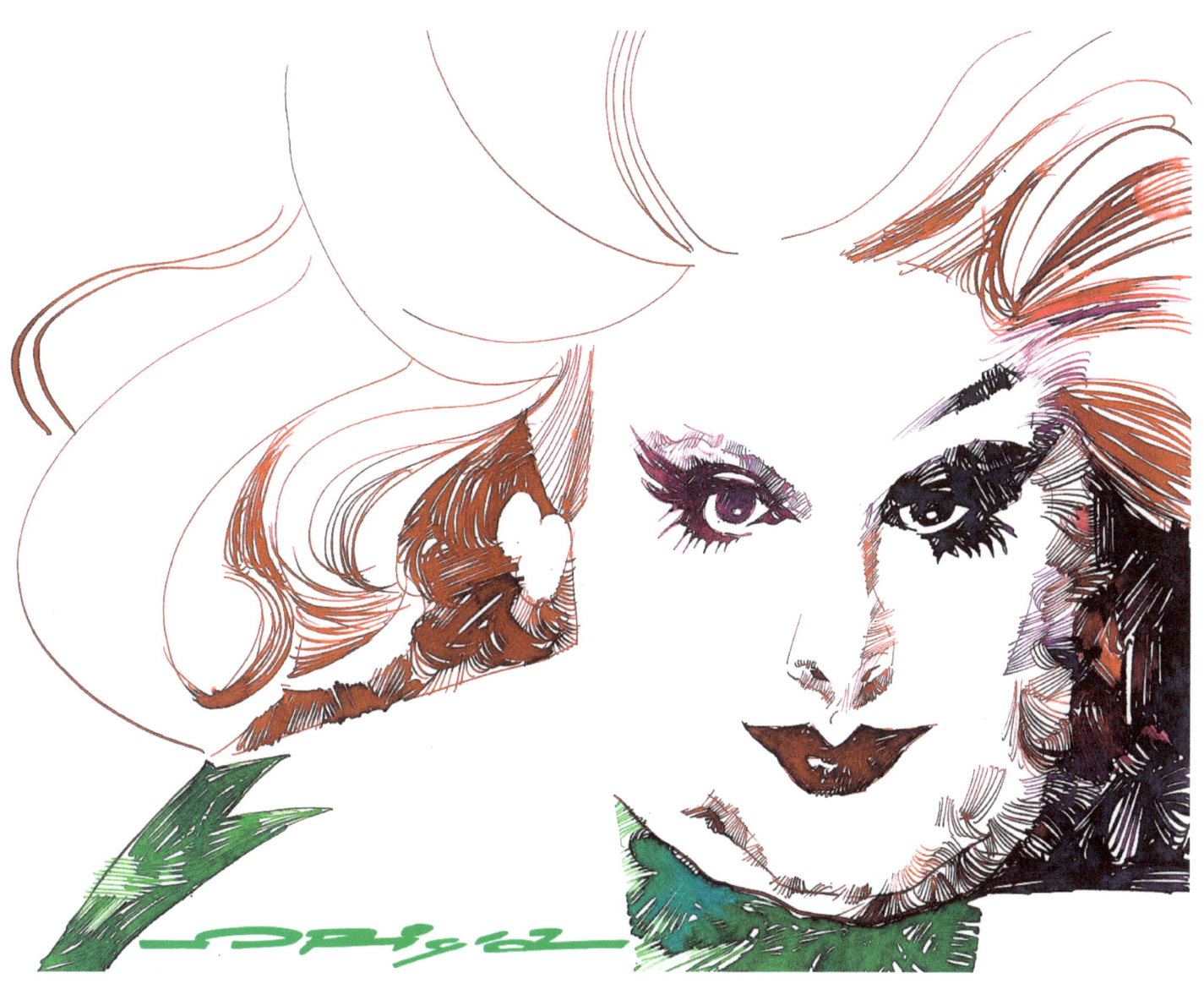

(13) Divine

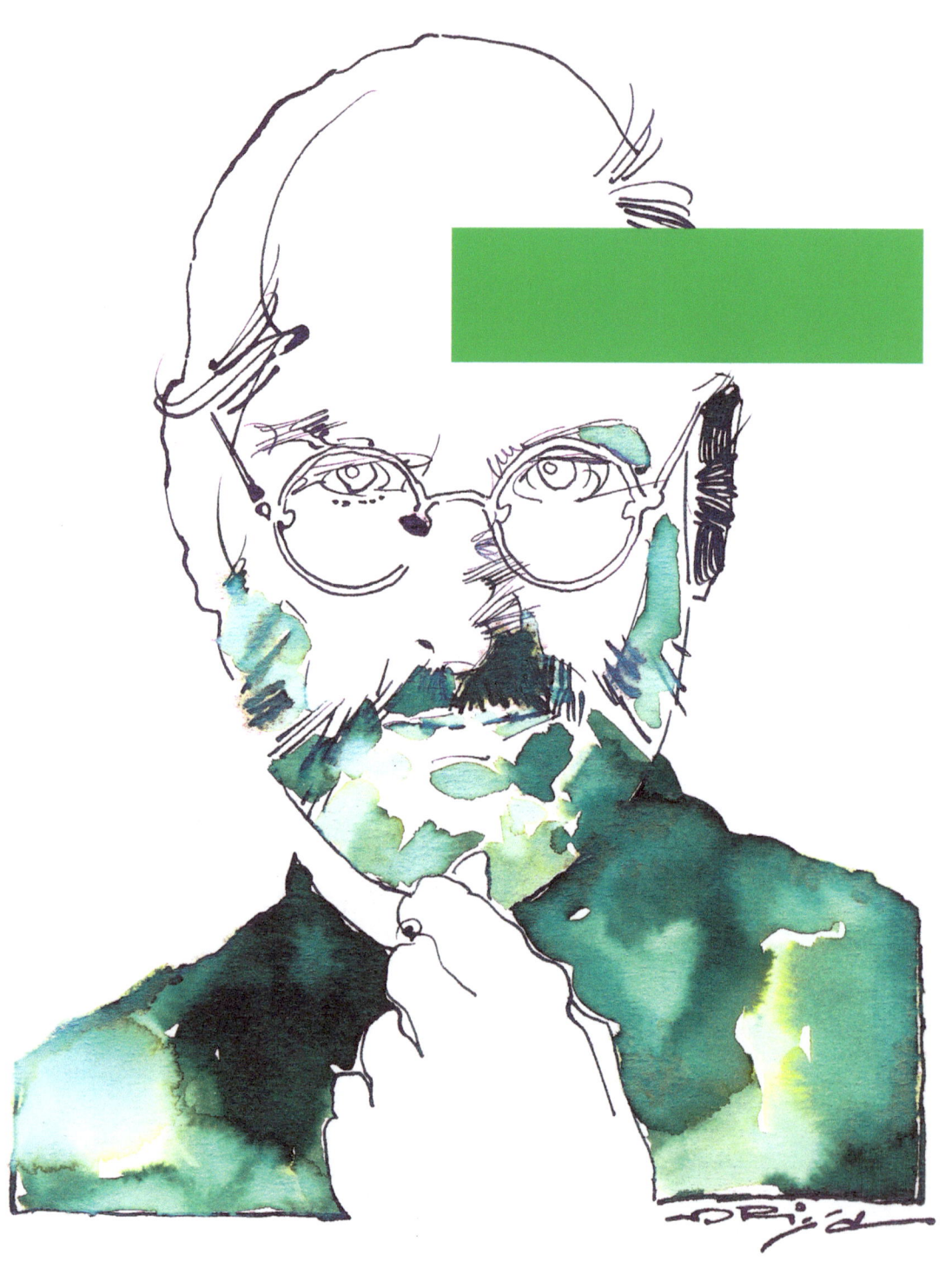

(14) Steve Jobs

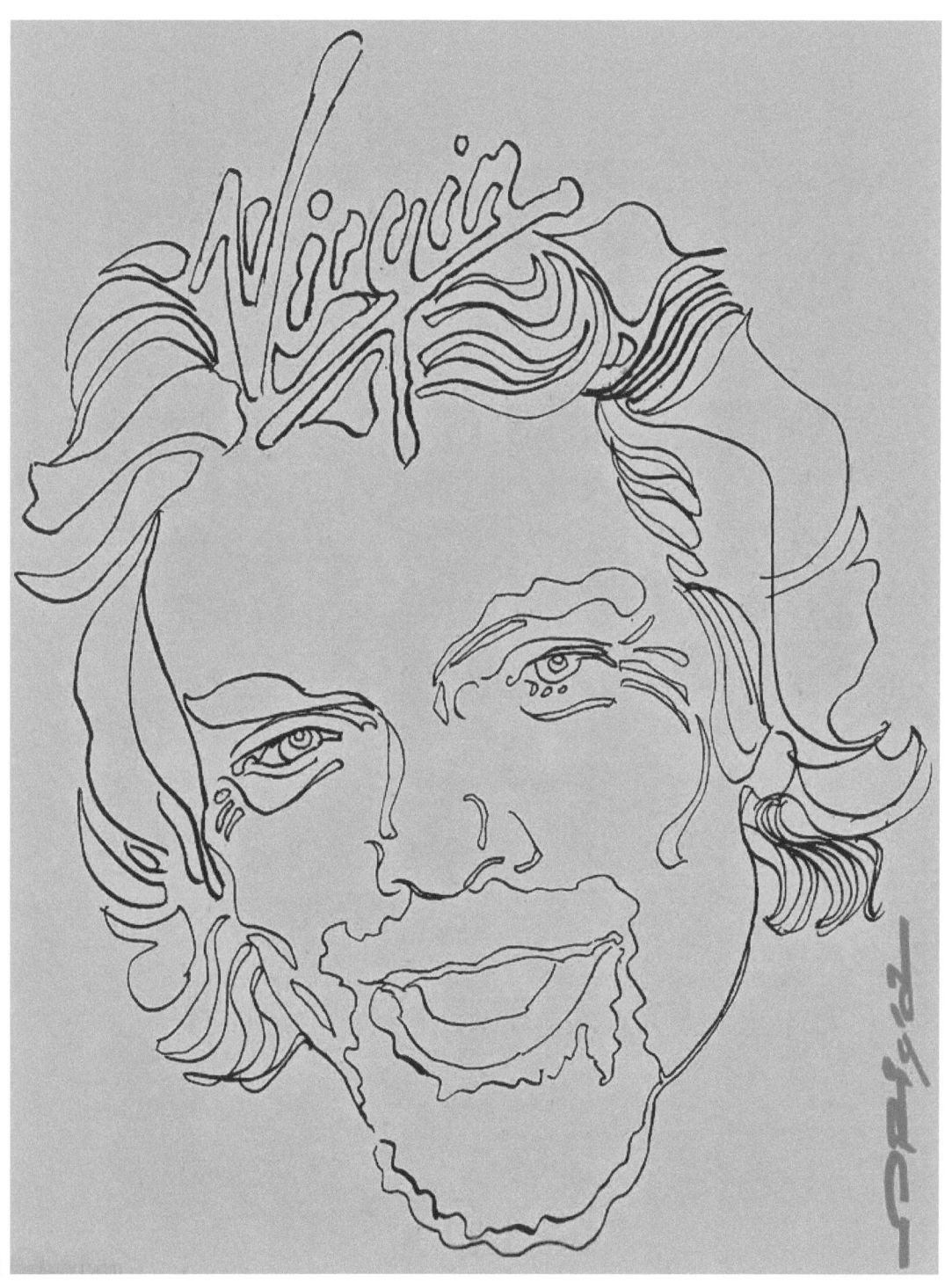

(15) Richard Branson

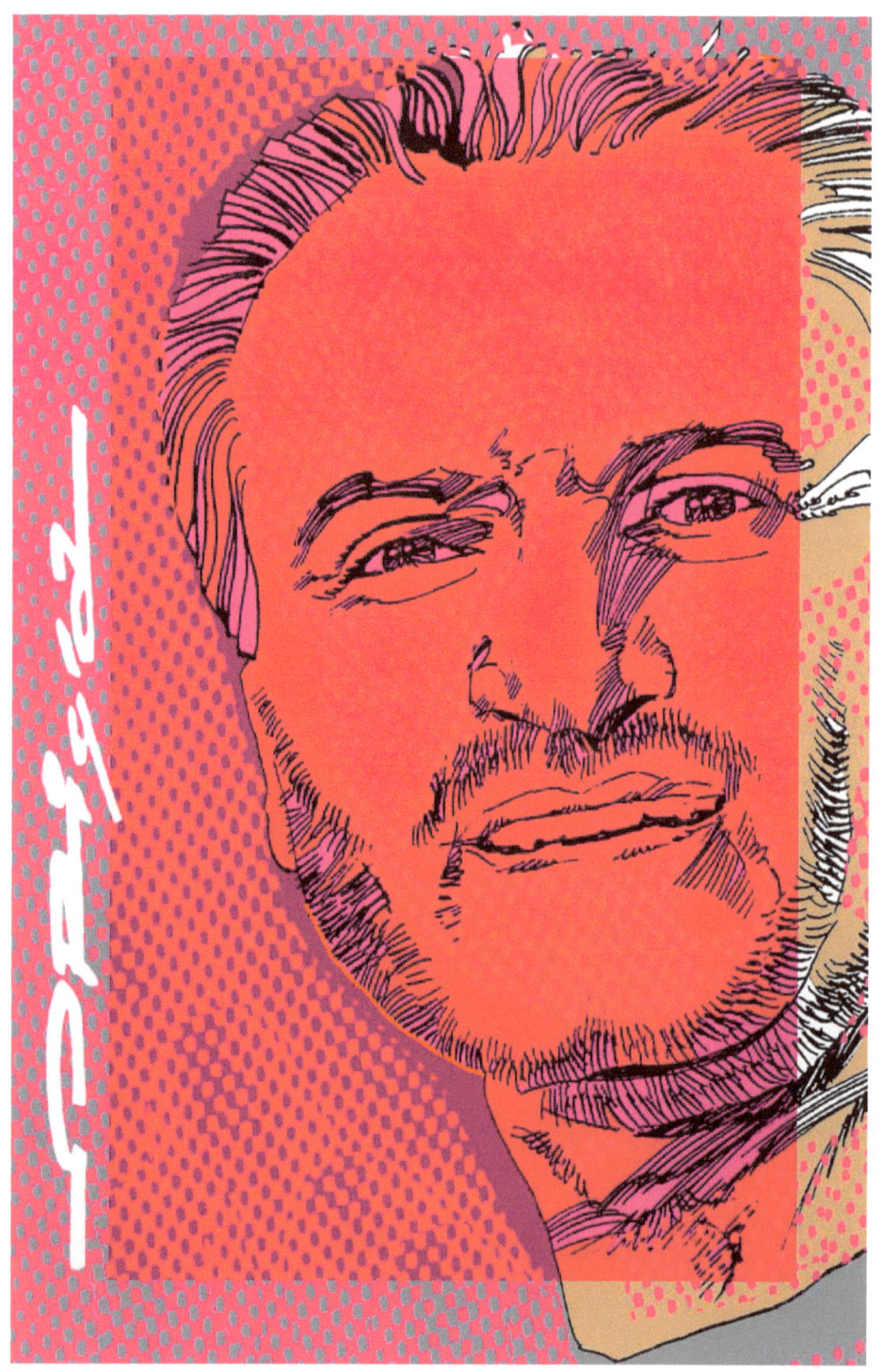

(16) Gianni Versace

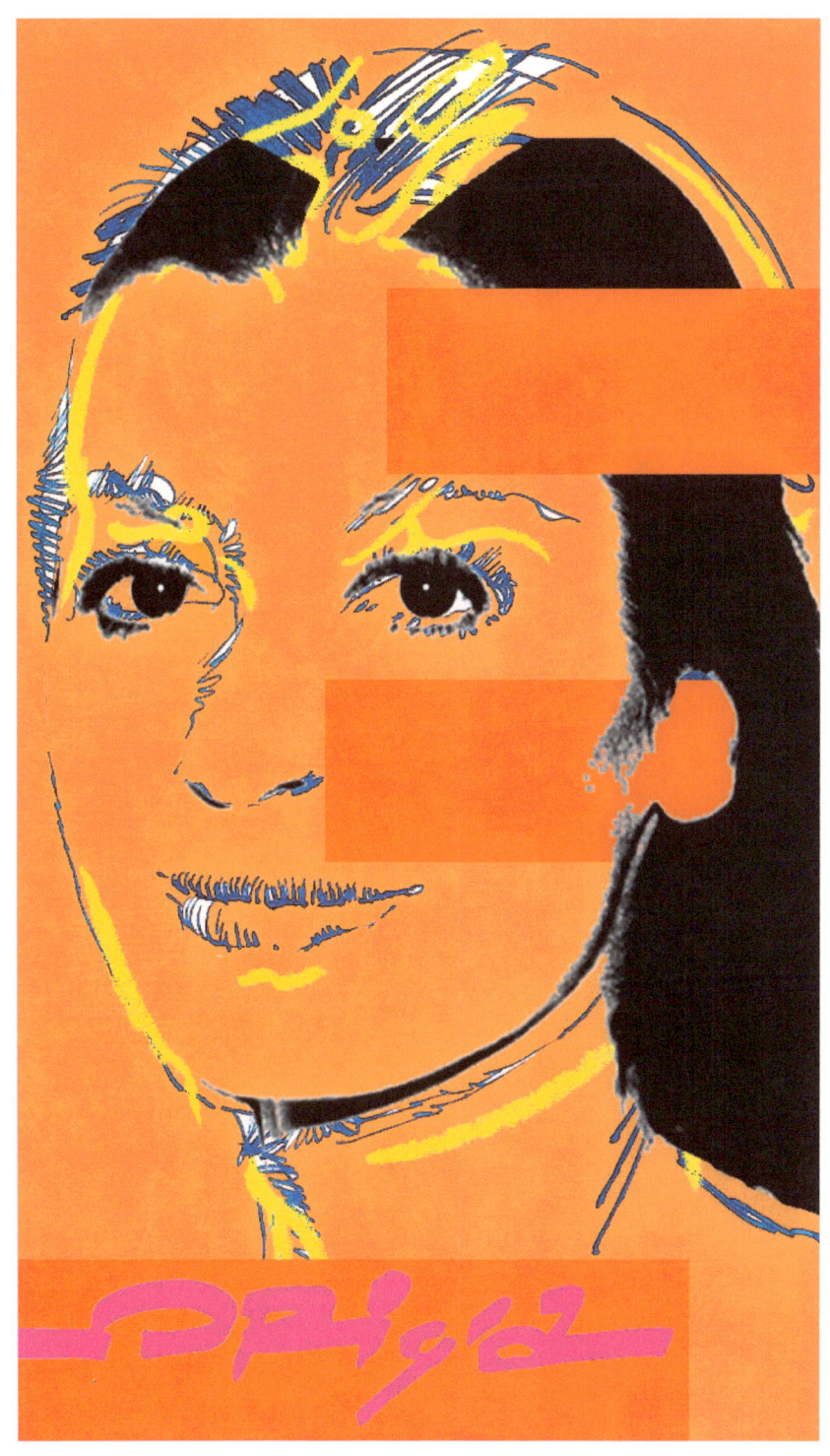

(17) Carla Fracci

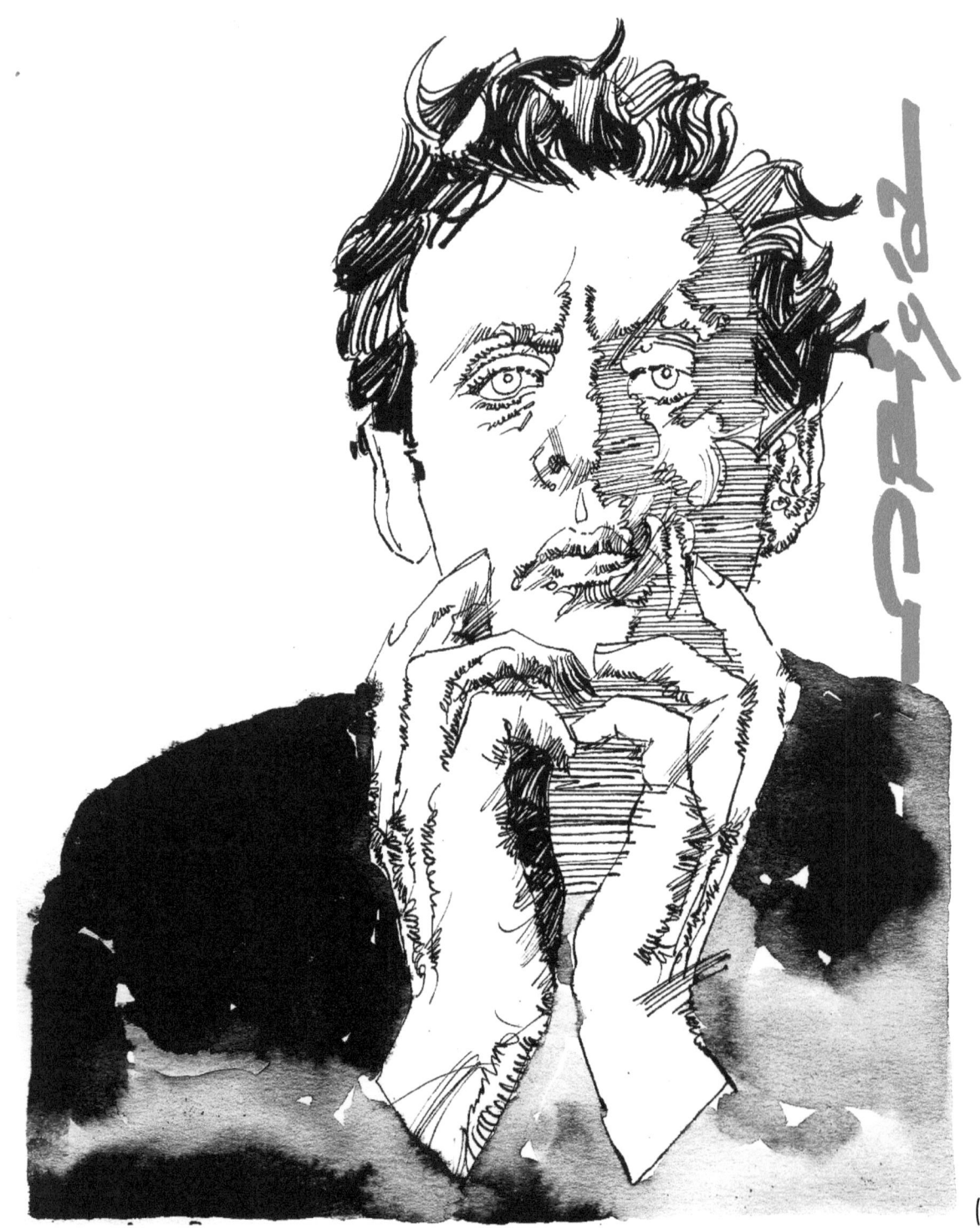

(18) Philip Glass

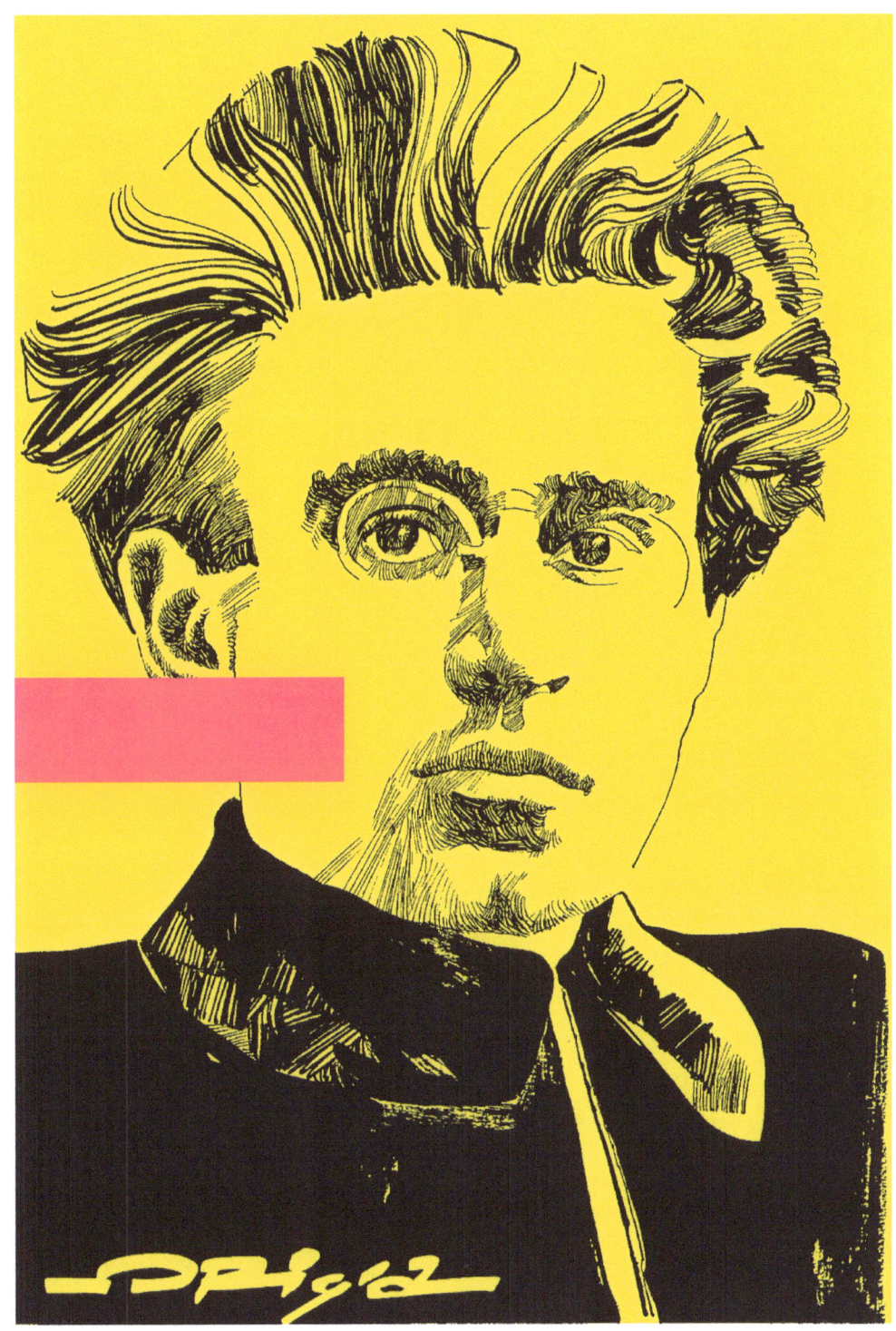

(19) Antonio Gramsci

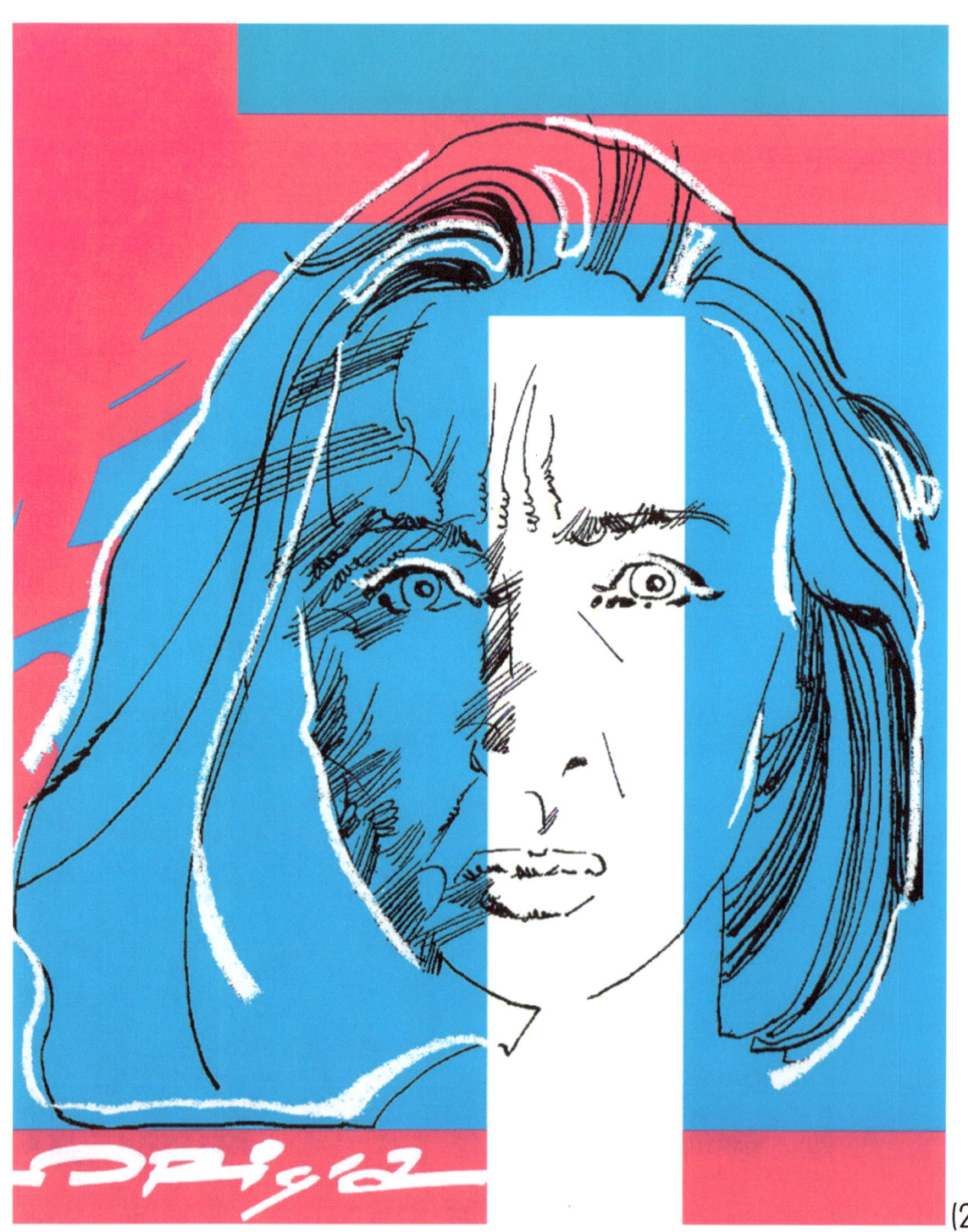

(20) Oriana Fallaci

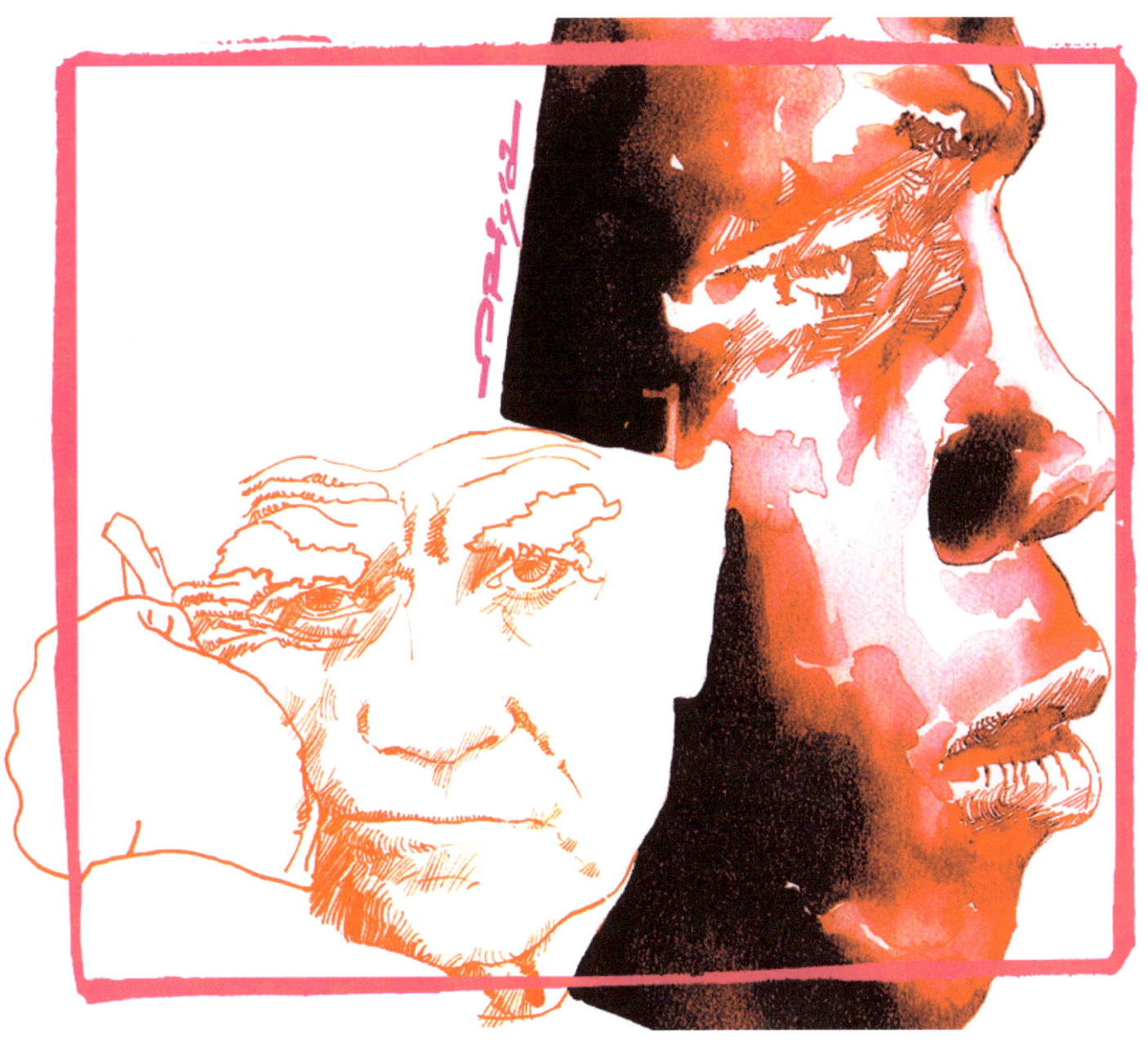

(21) Alberto Moravia

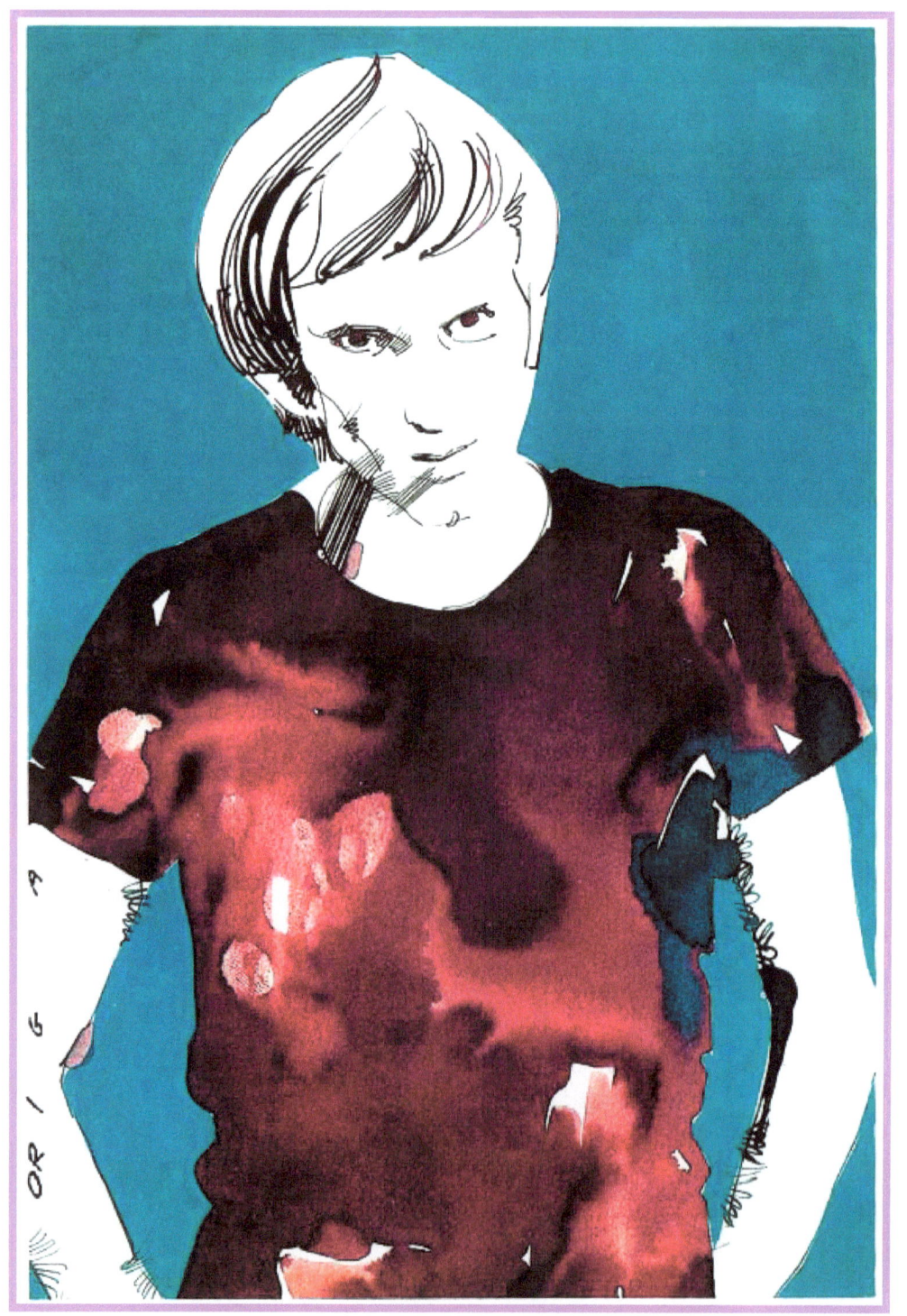

(22) Dario Argento

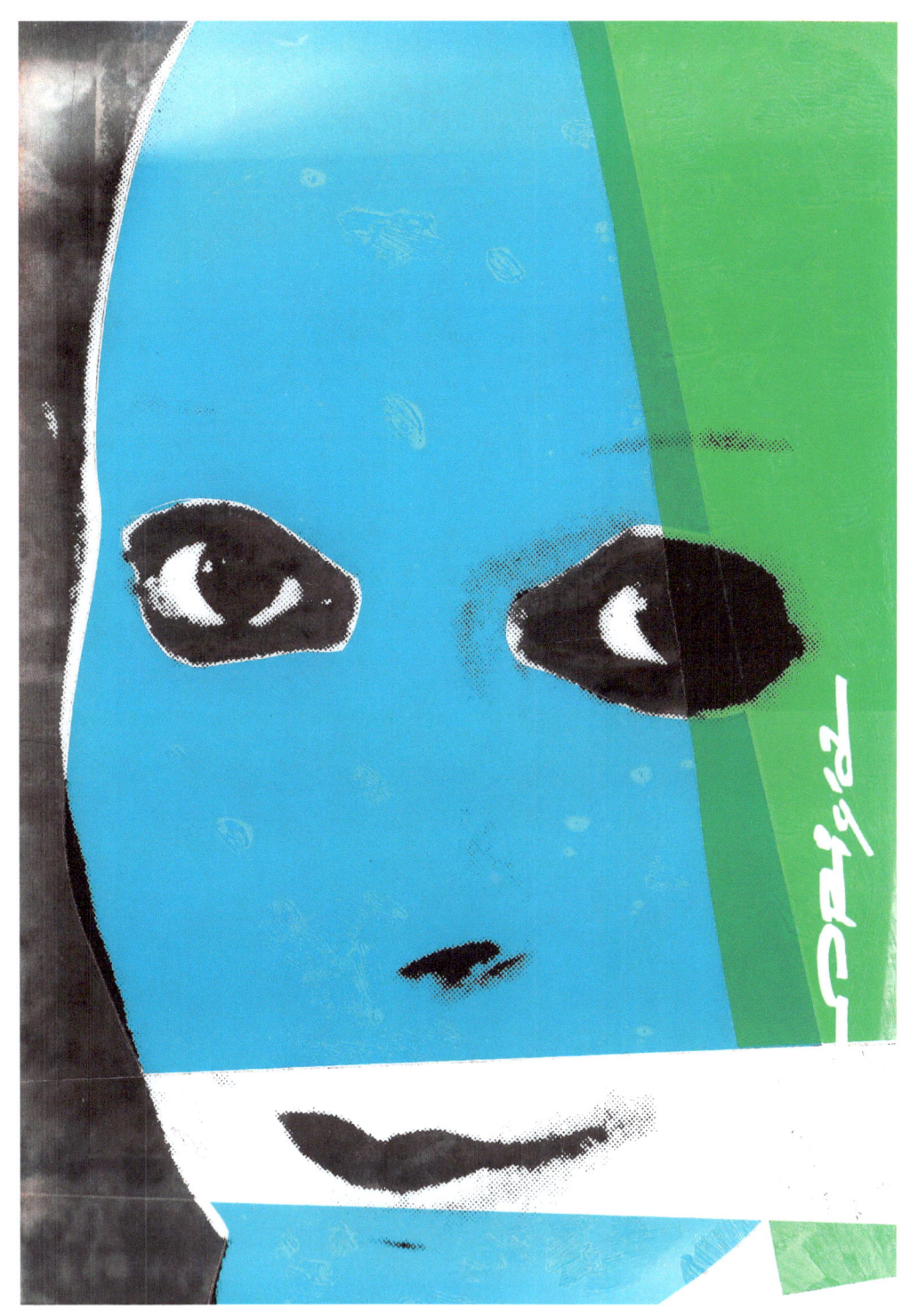

(23) Lindsay Kemp

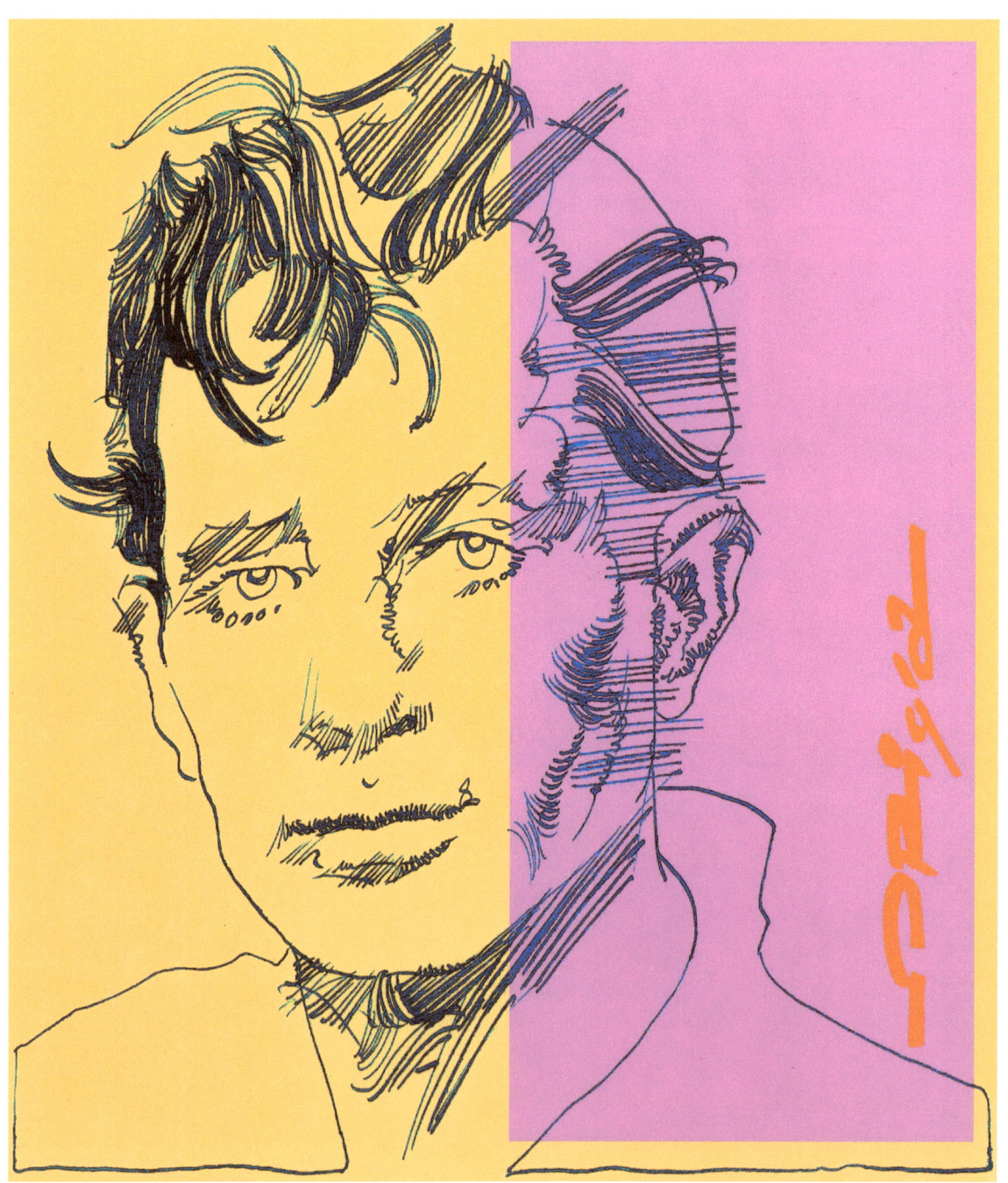

(24) Jack Kerouac

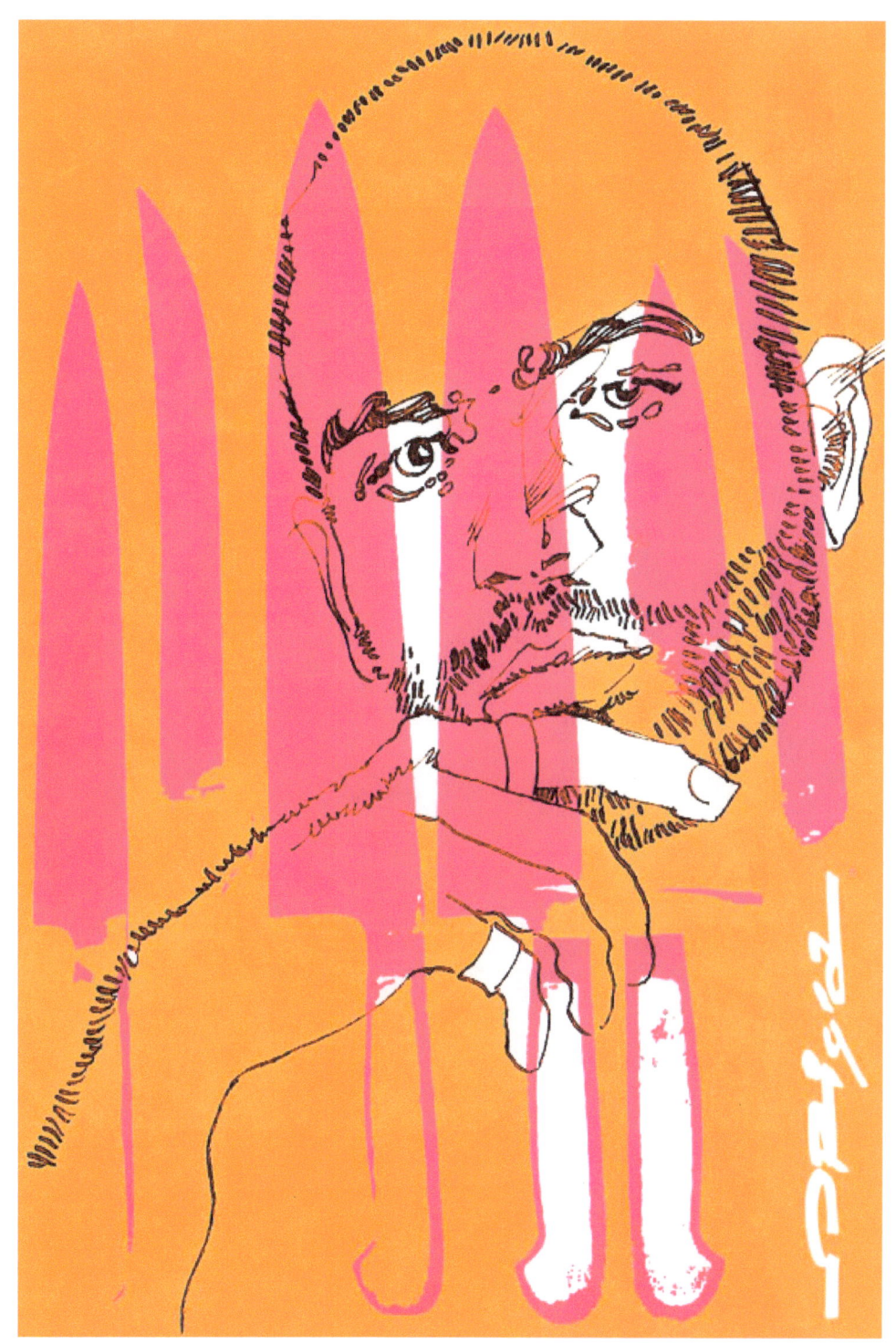

(25) Roberto Saviano

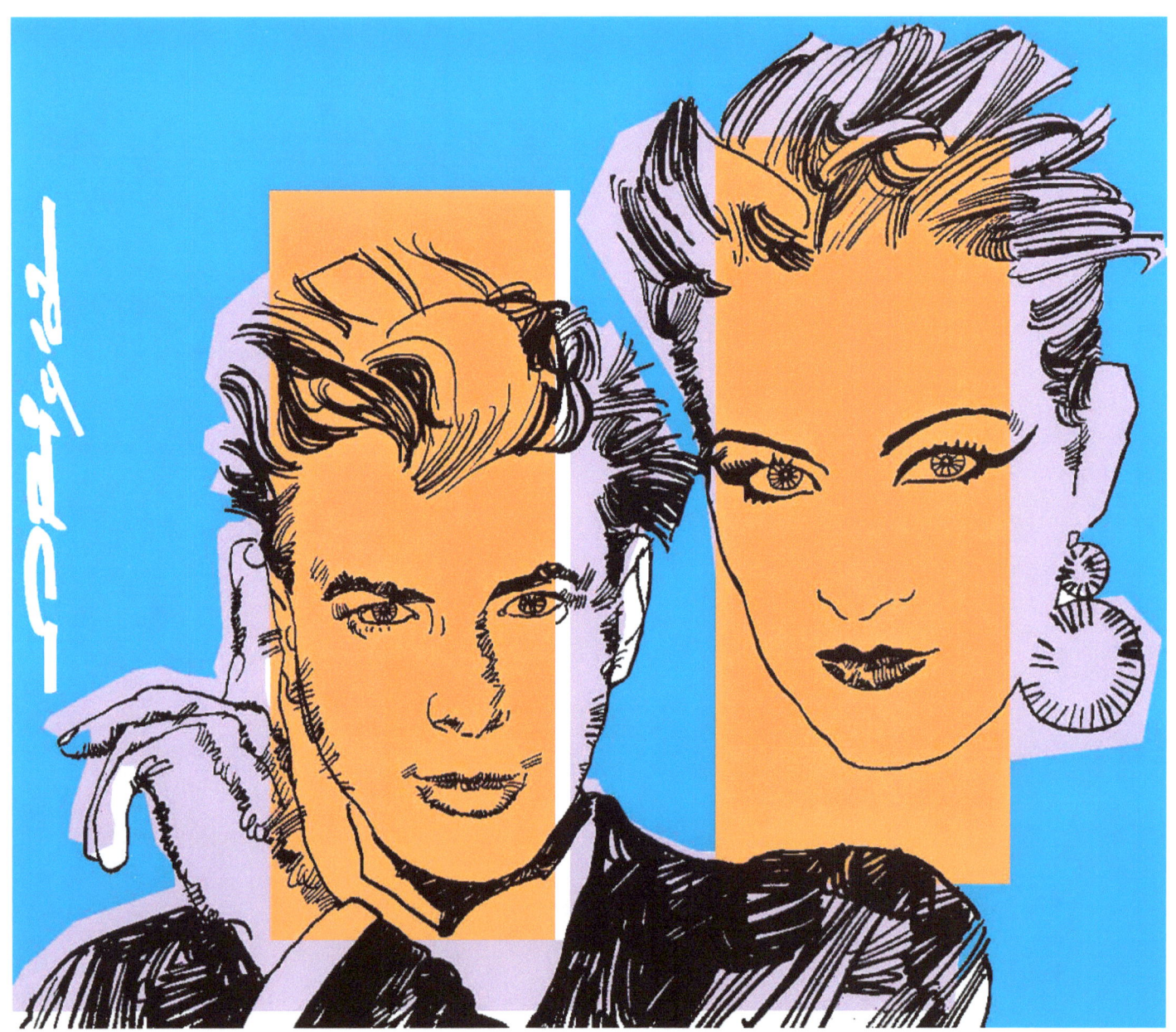

(26) Krisma

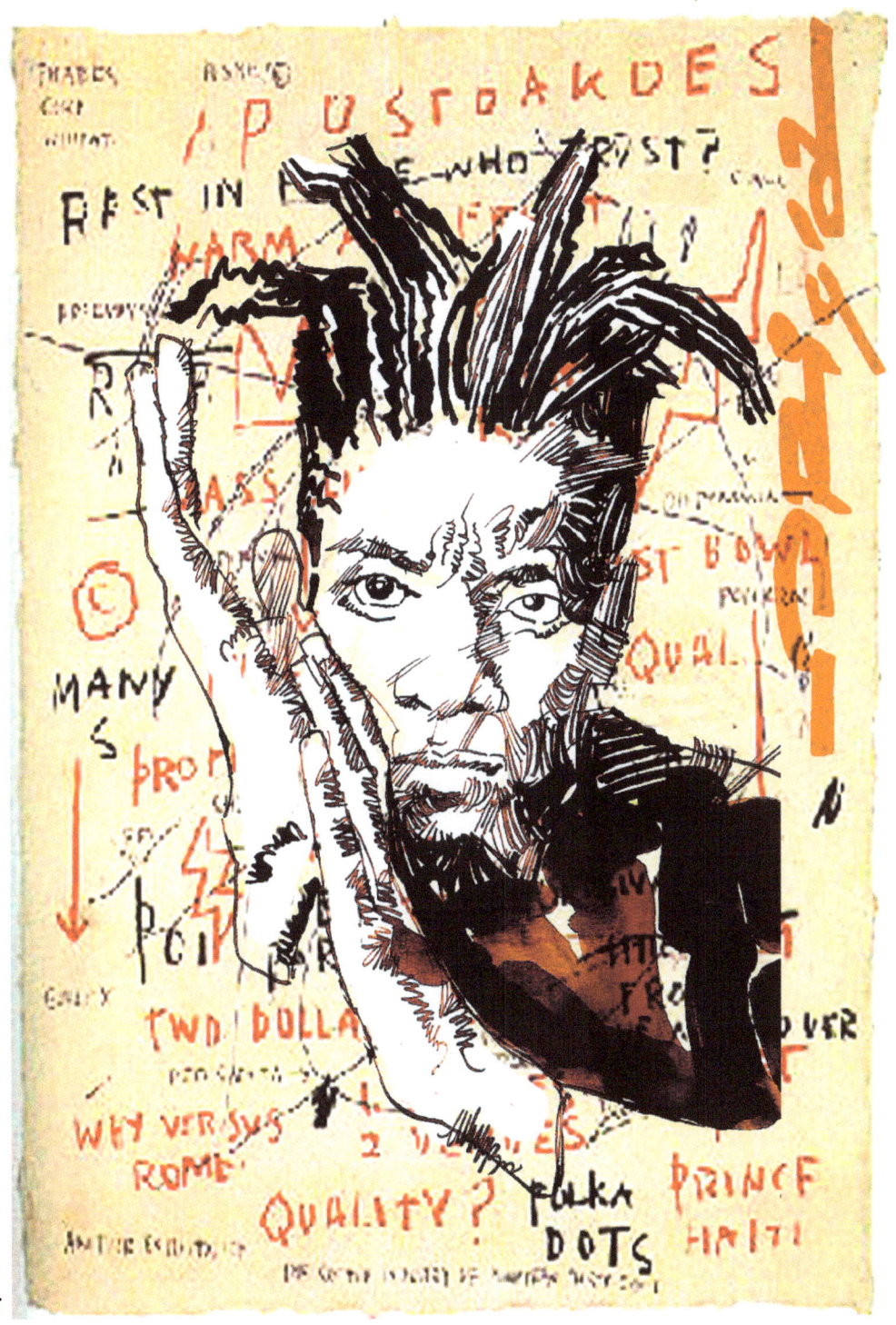

(27) Jean-Michel Basquiat

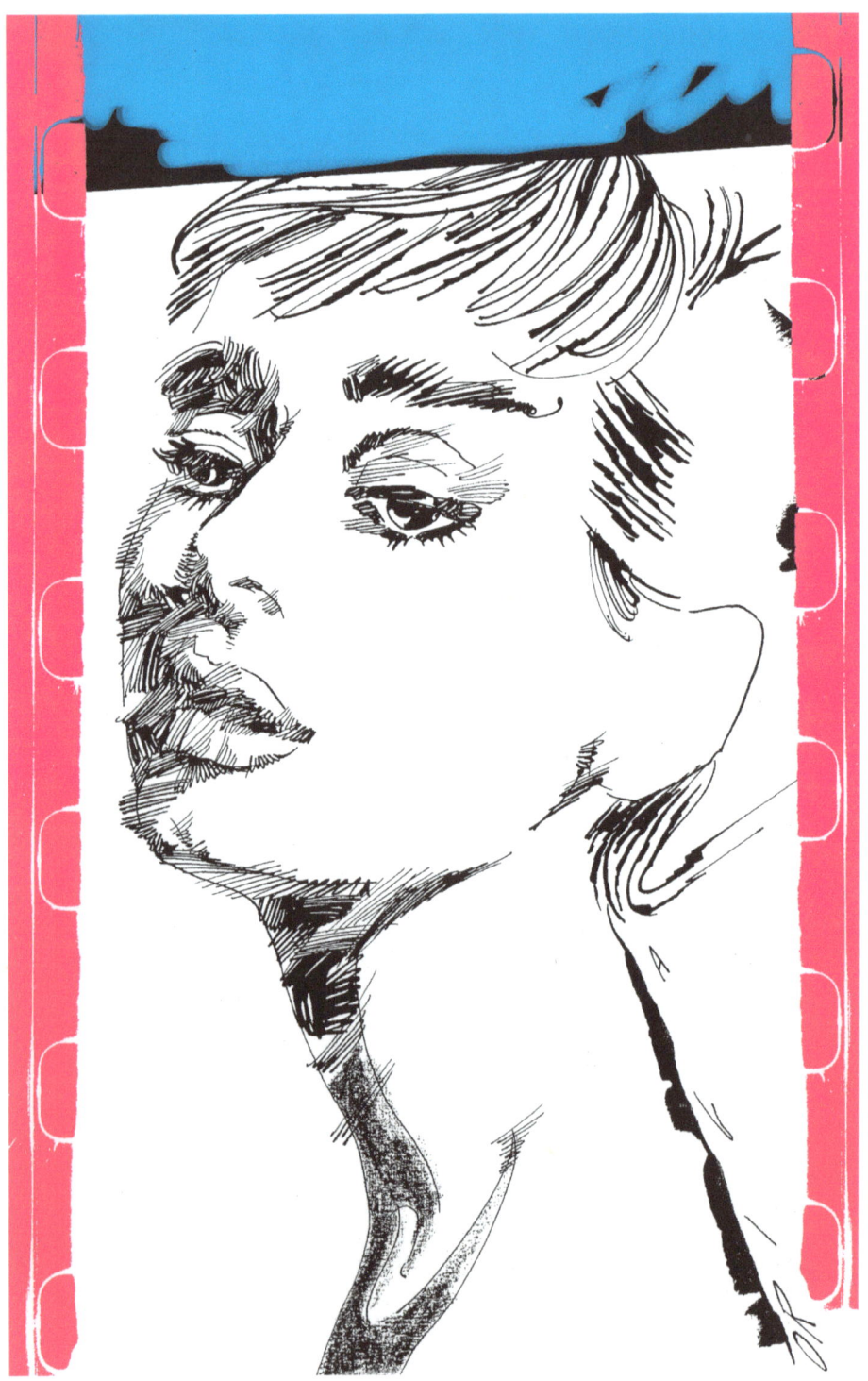

(28) Audrey Hepburn

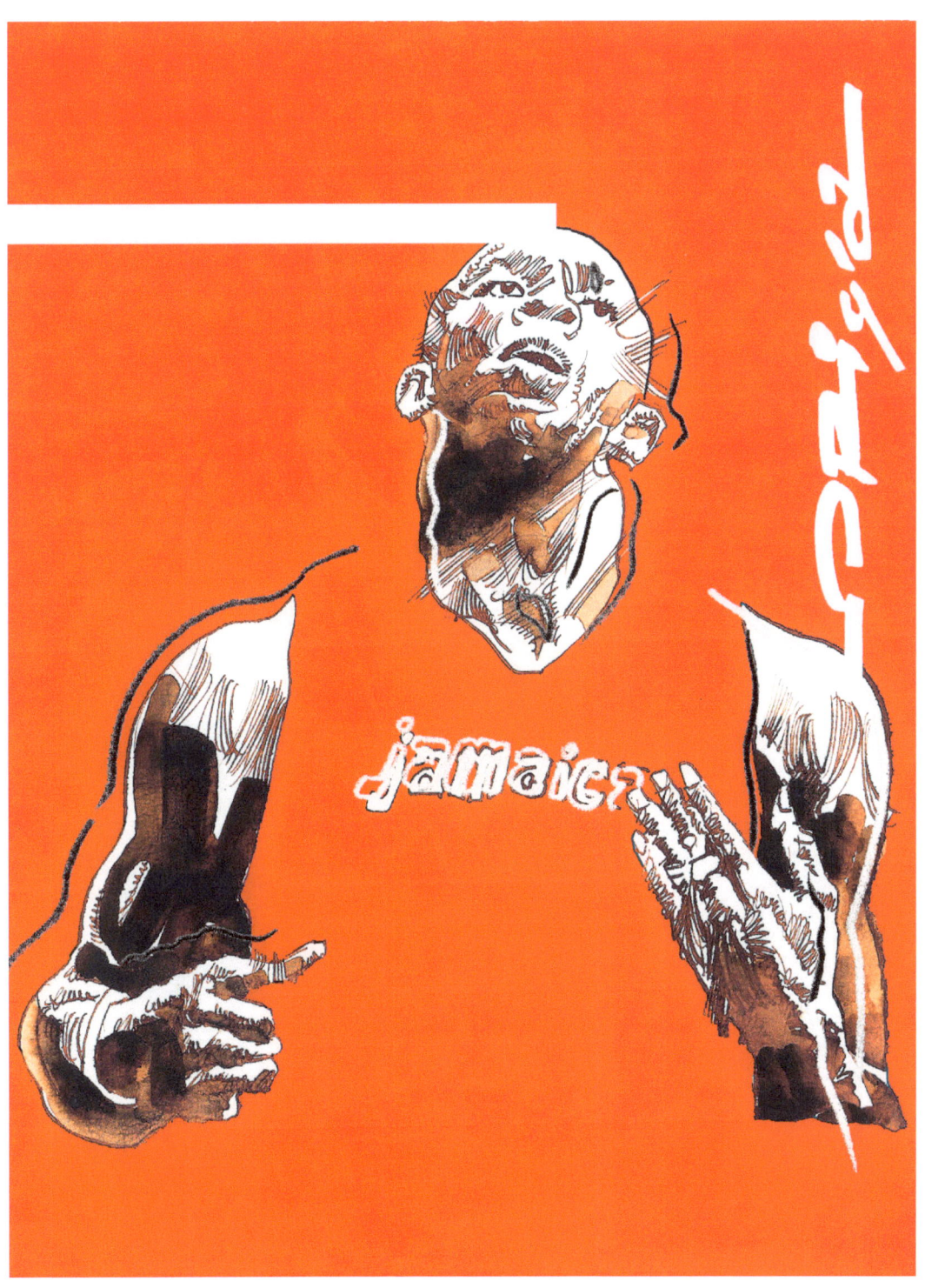

(29) Usain Bolt

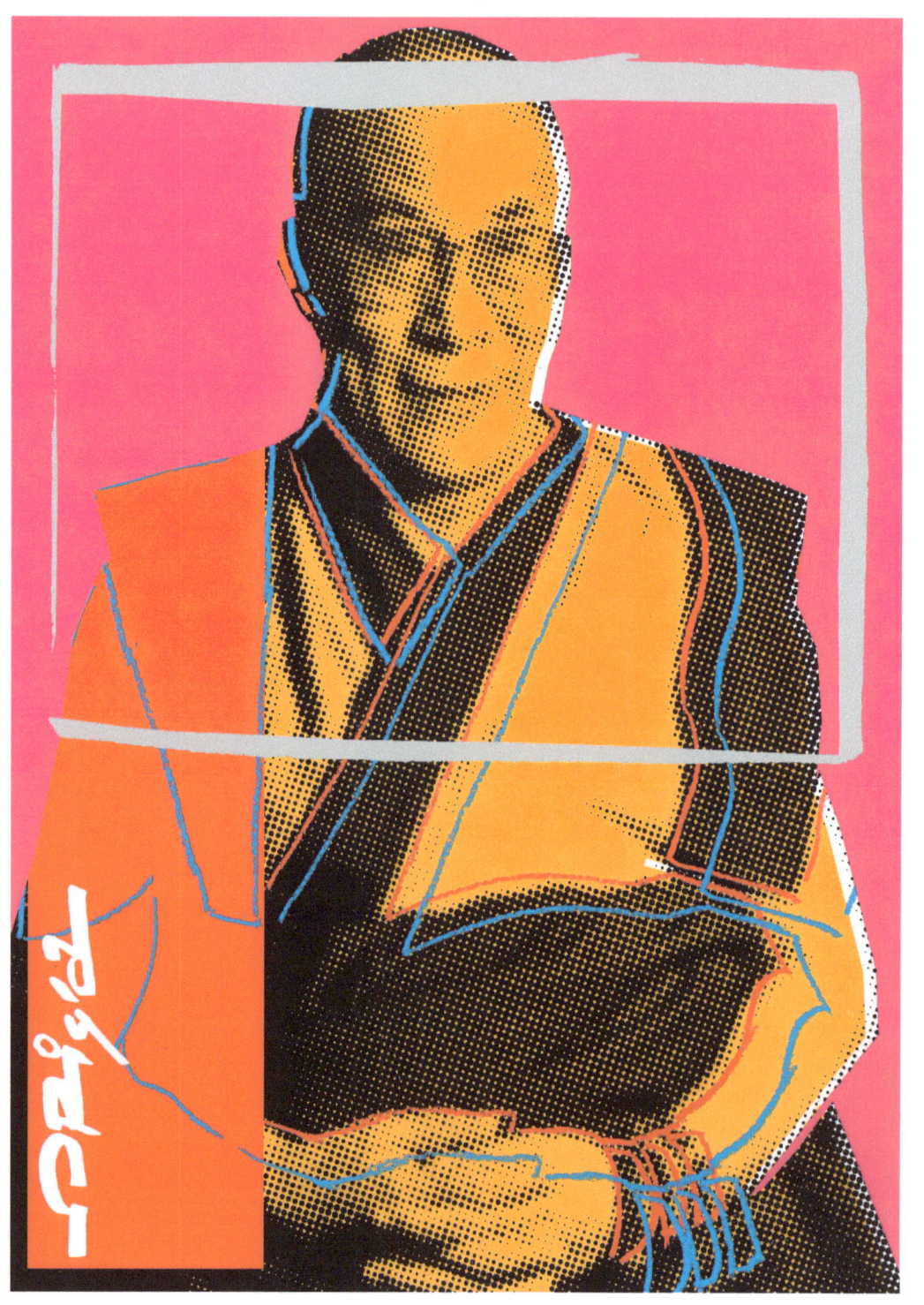

(30) Dalai Lama

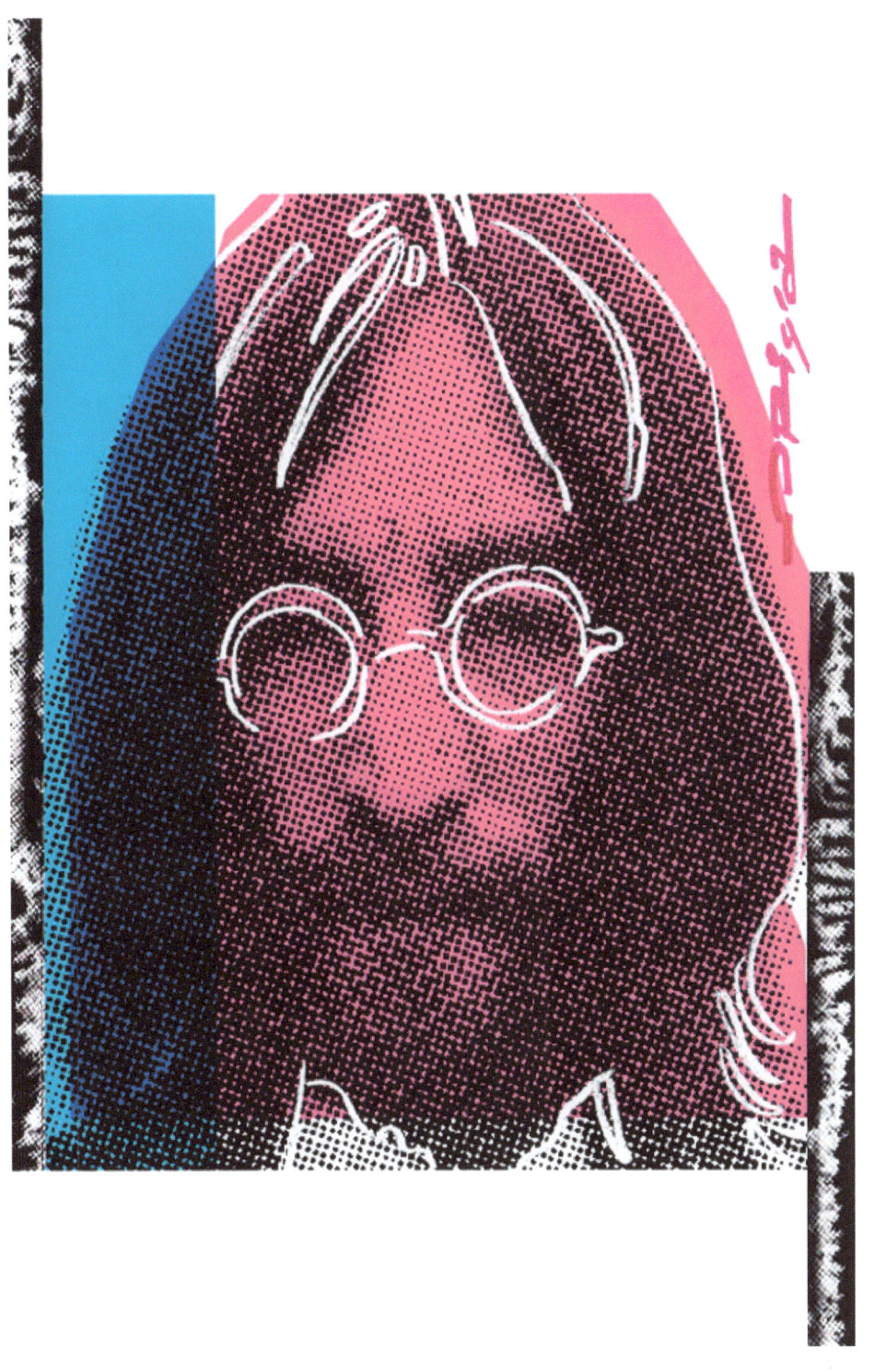

(31) John Lennon

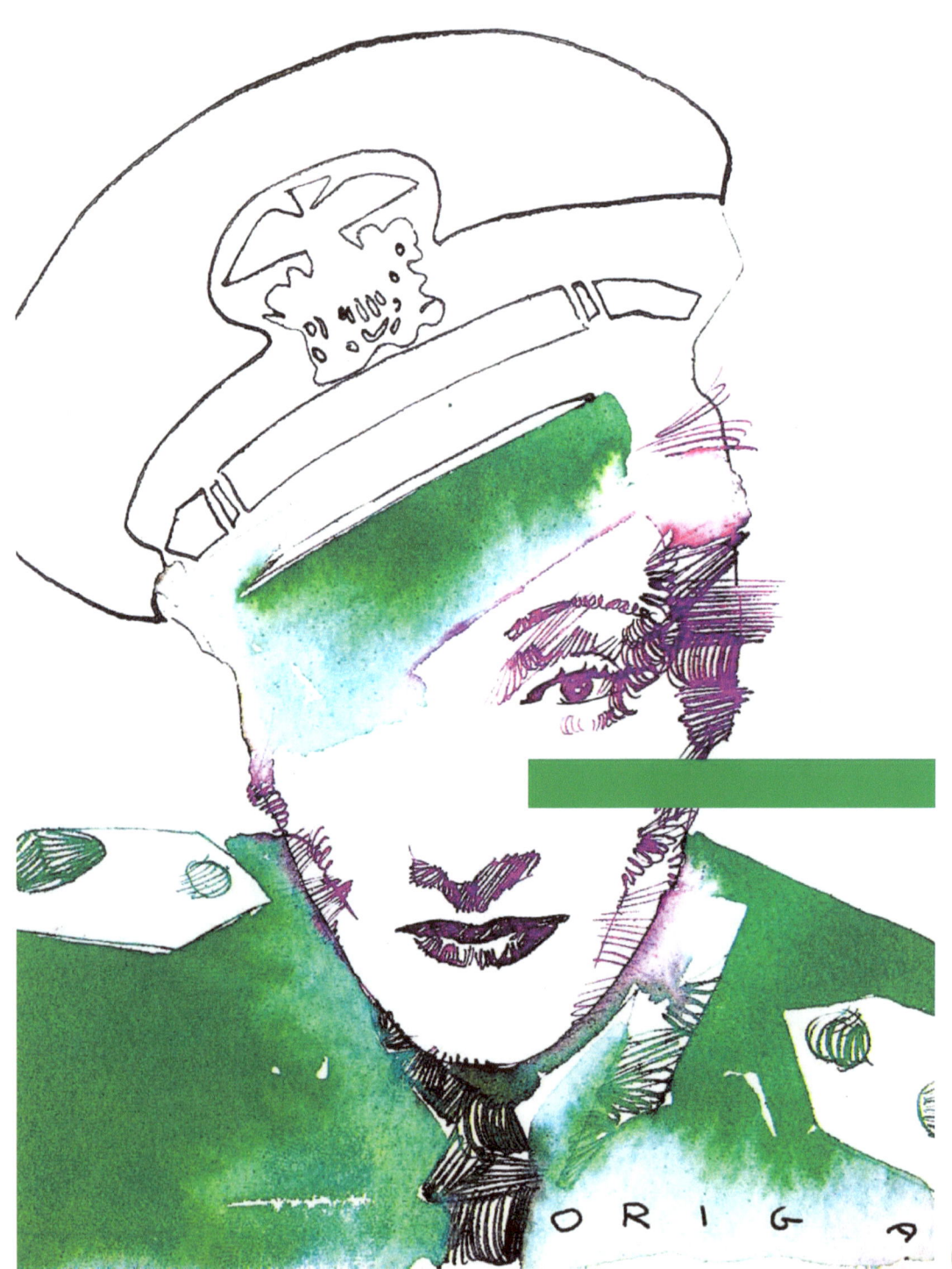

ORIGA

(32) Marlene Dietrich

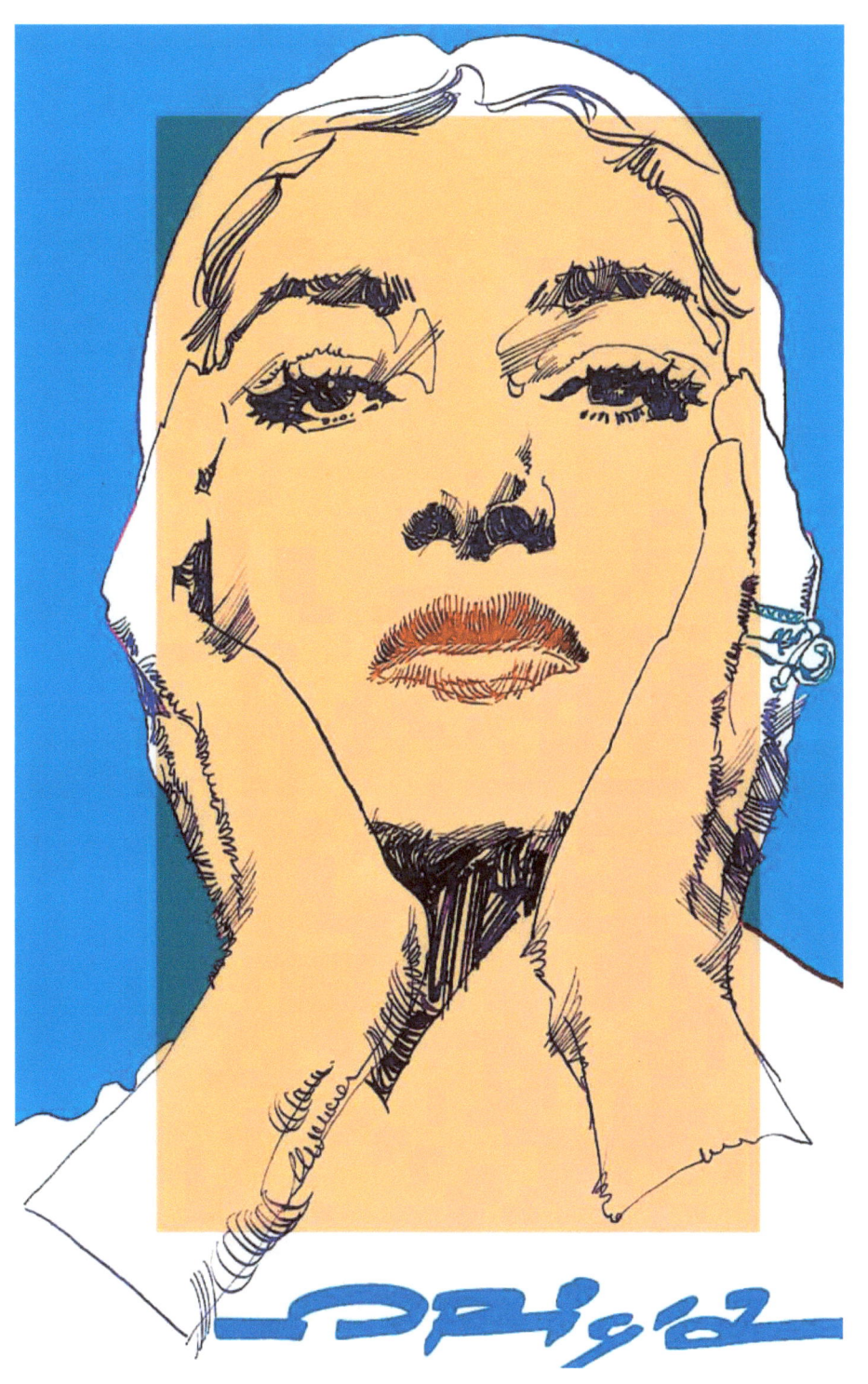

(33) Maria Callas

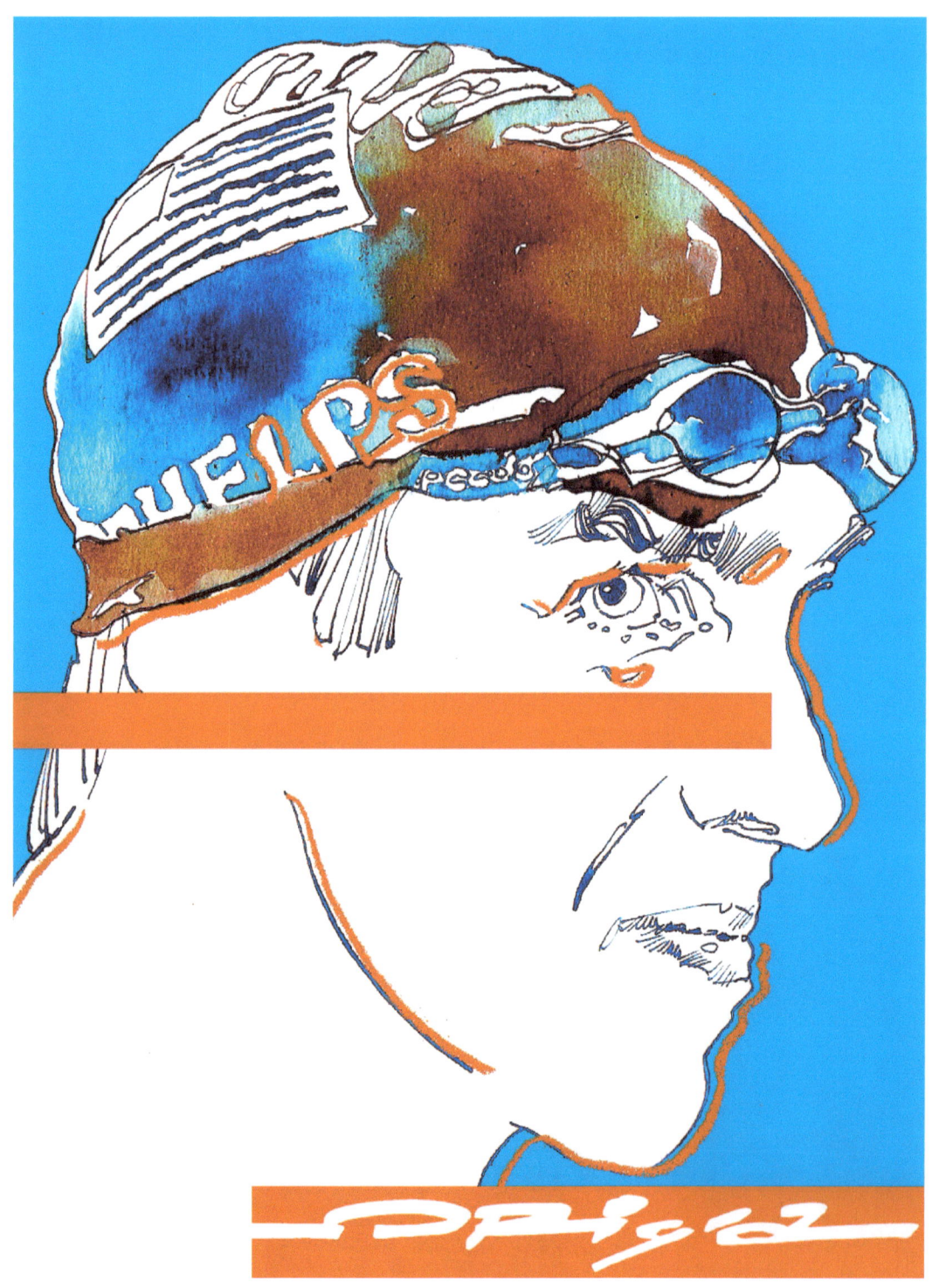

(34) Michael Phelps

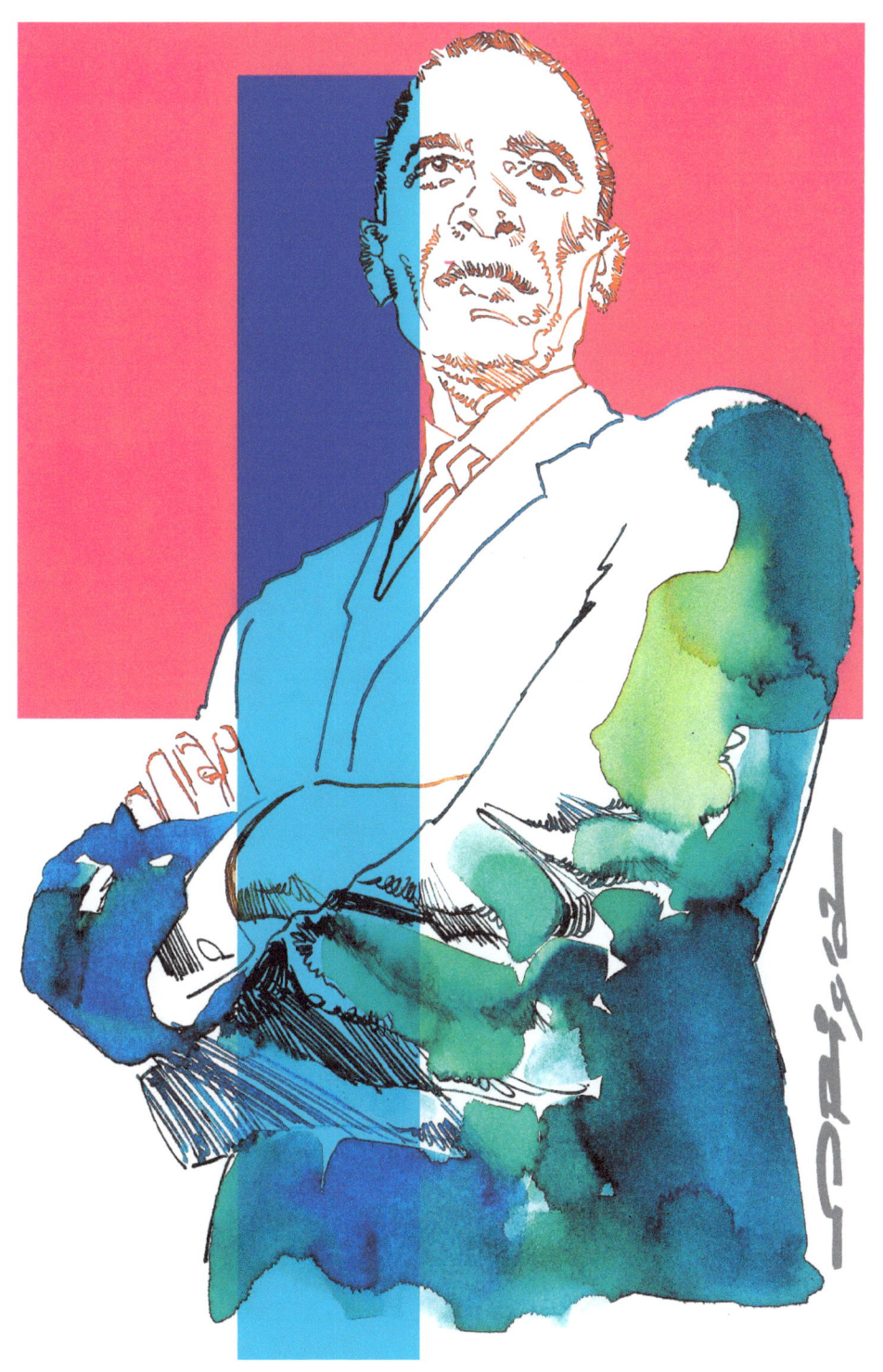

(35) Barack Obama

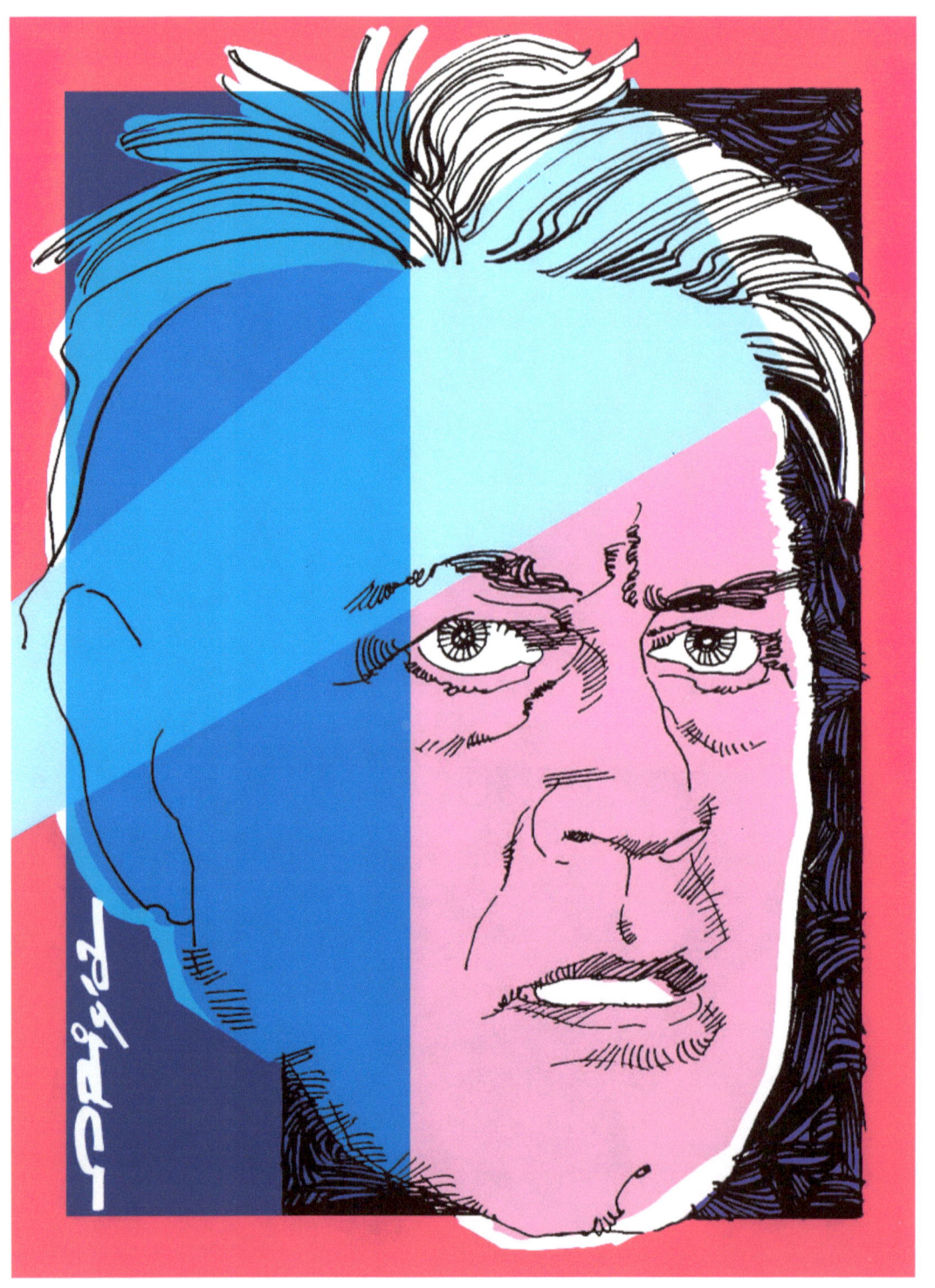

(36) Hugo Pratt

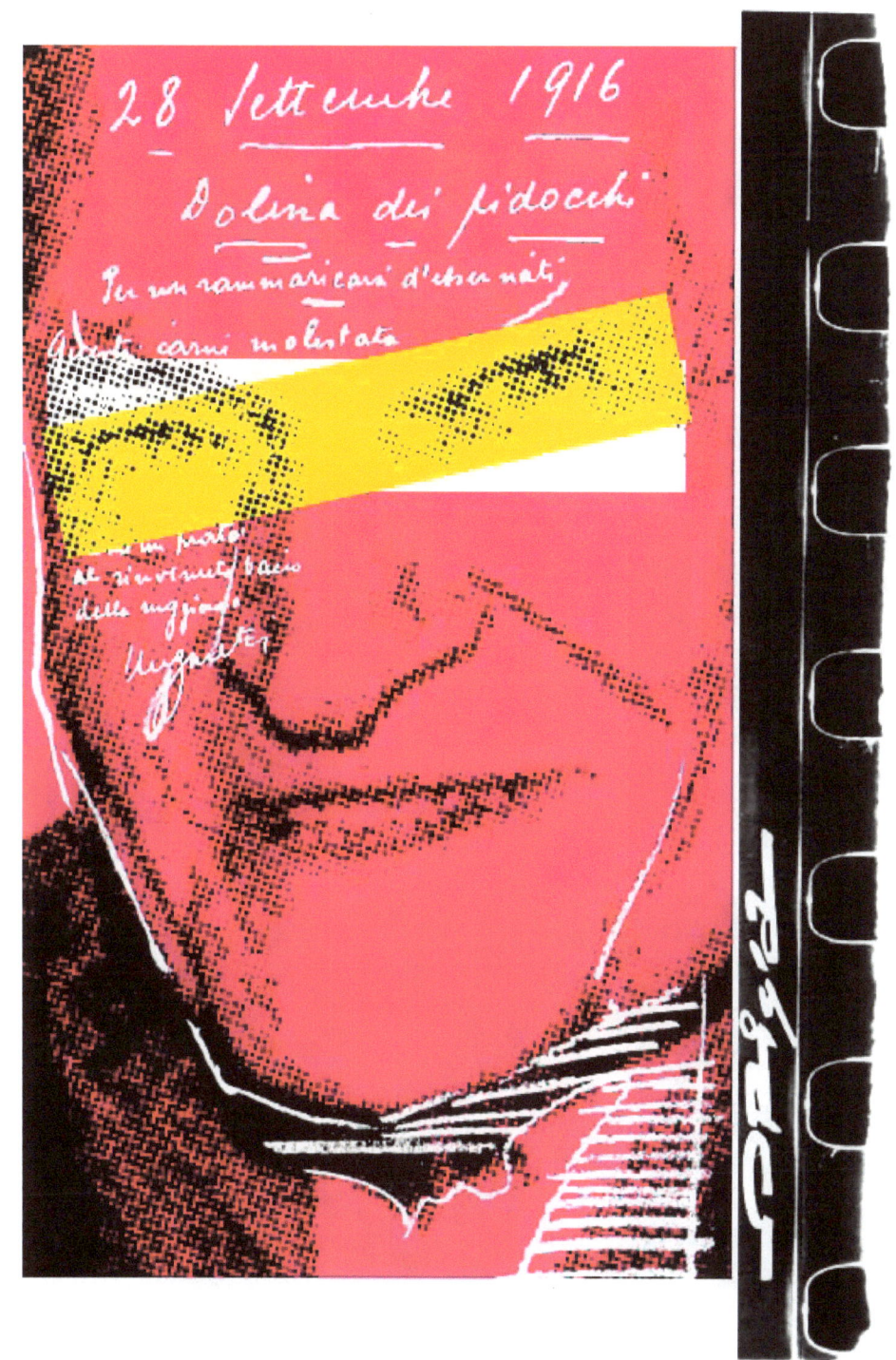

(37) Giuseppe Ungaretti

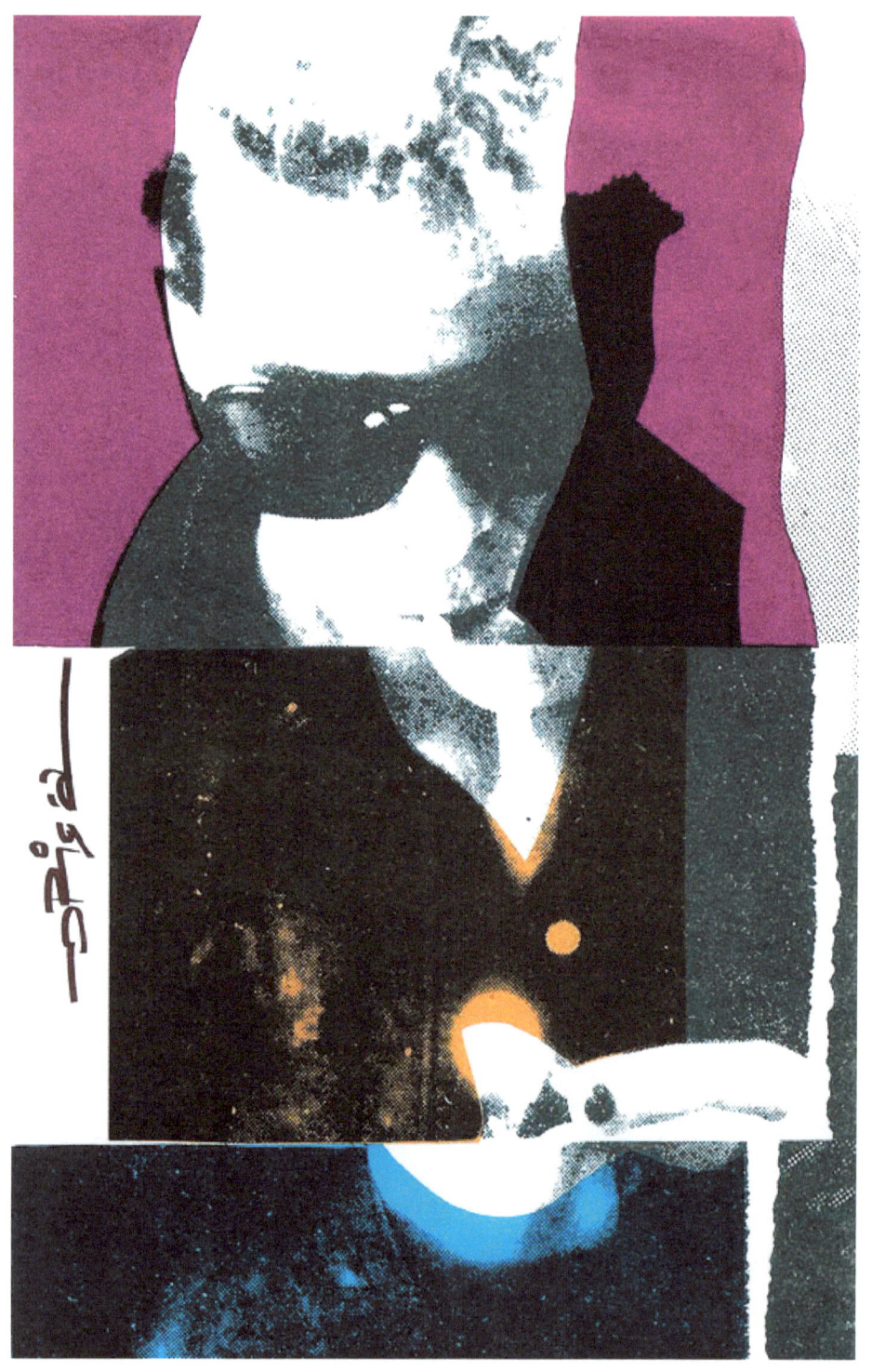

(38) Lou Reed

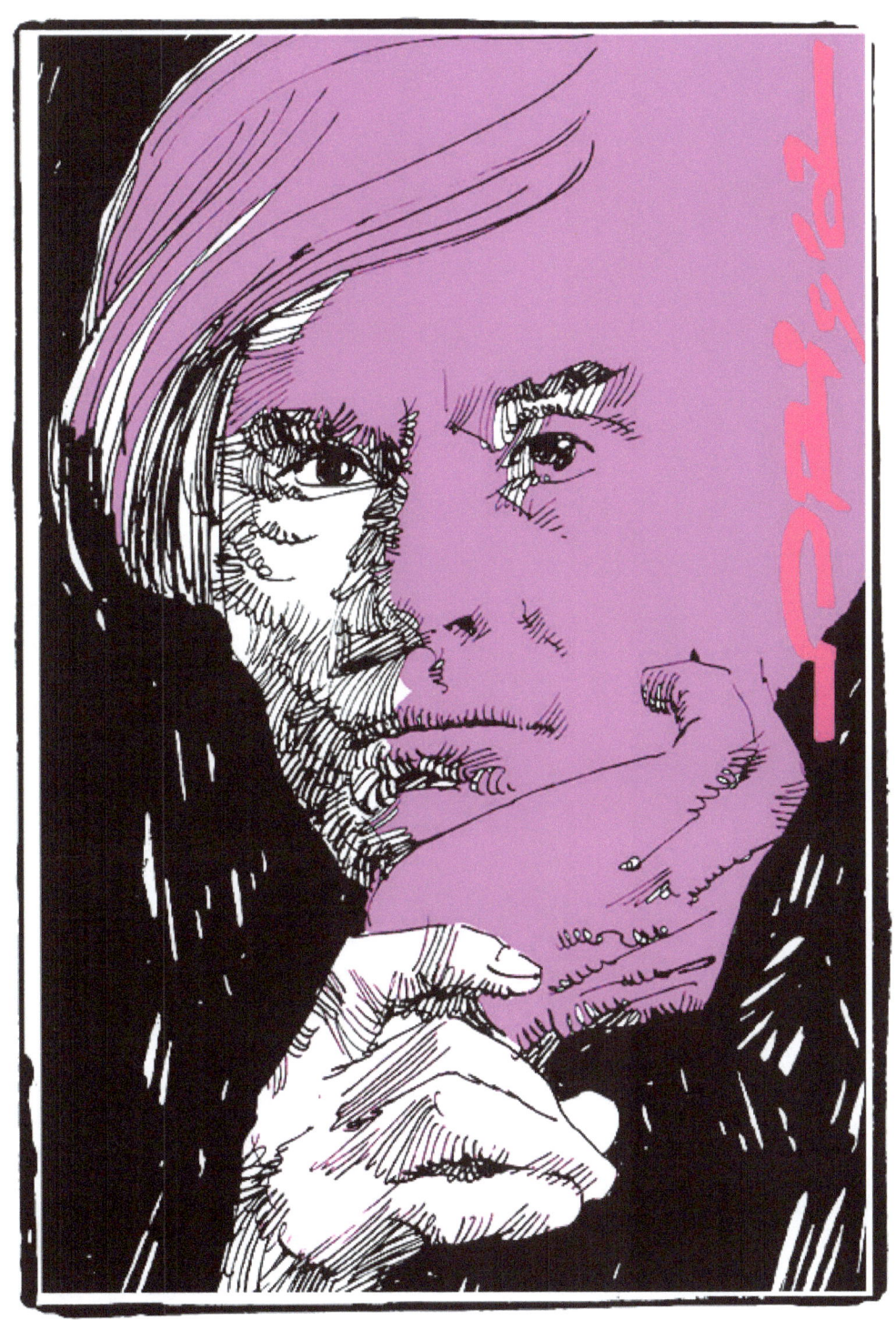

(39) Andy Warhol

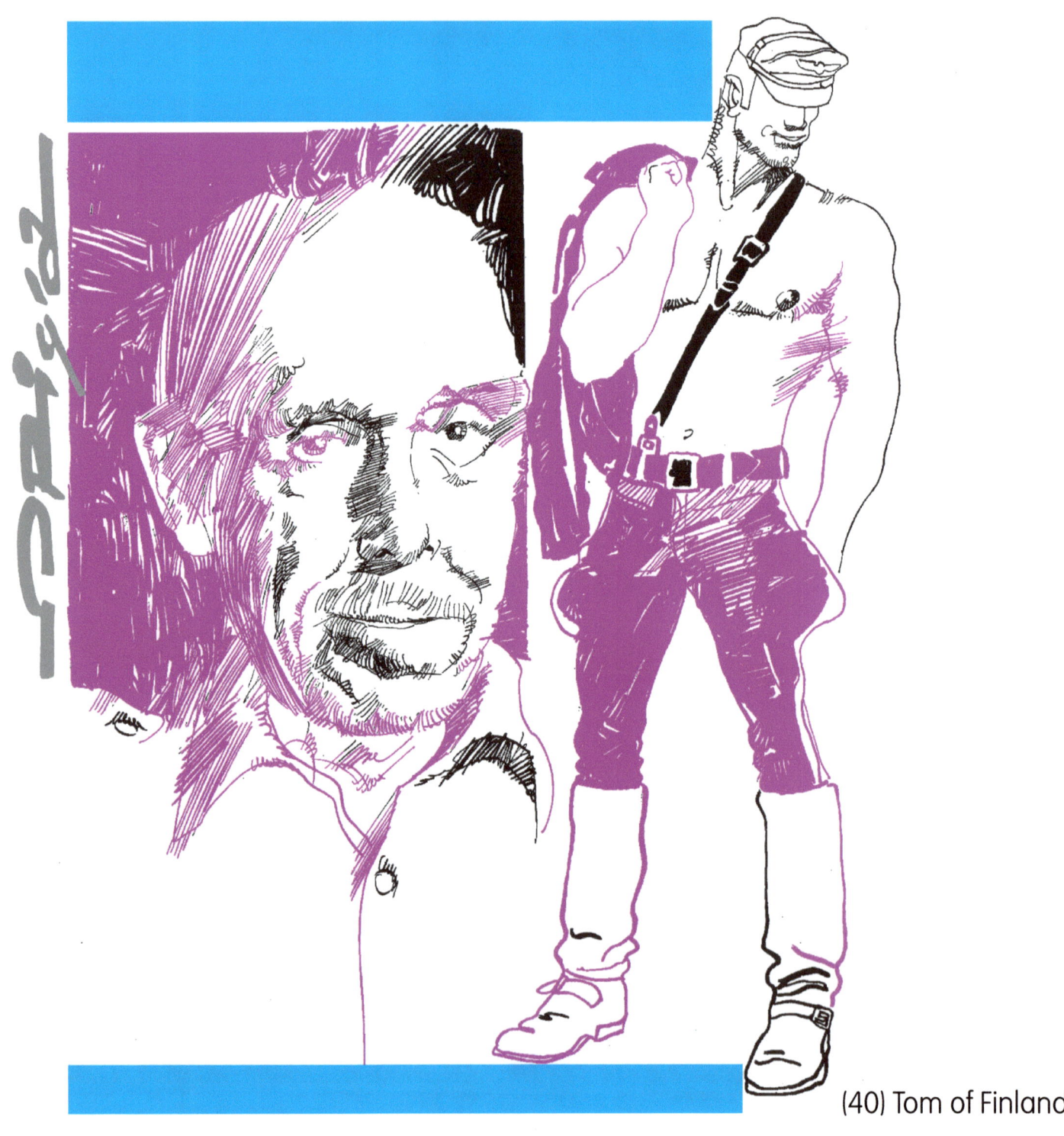

(40) Tom of Finland

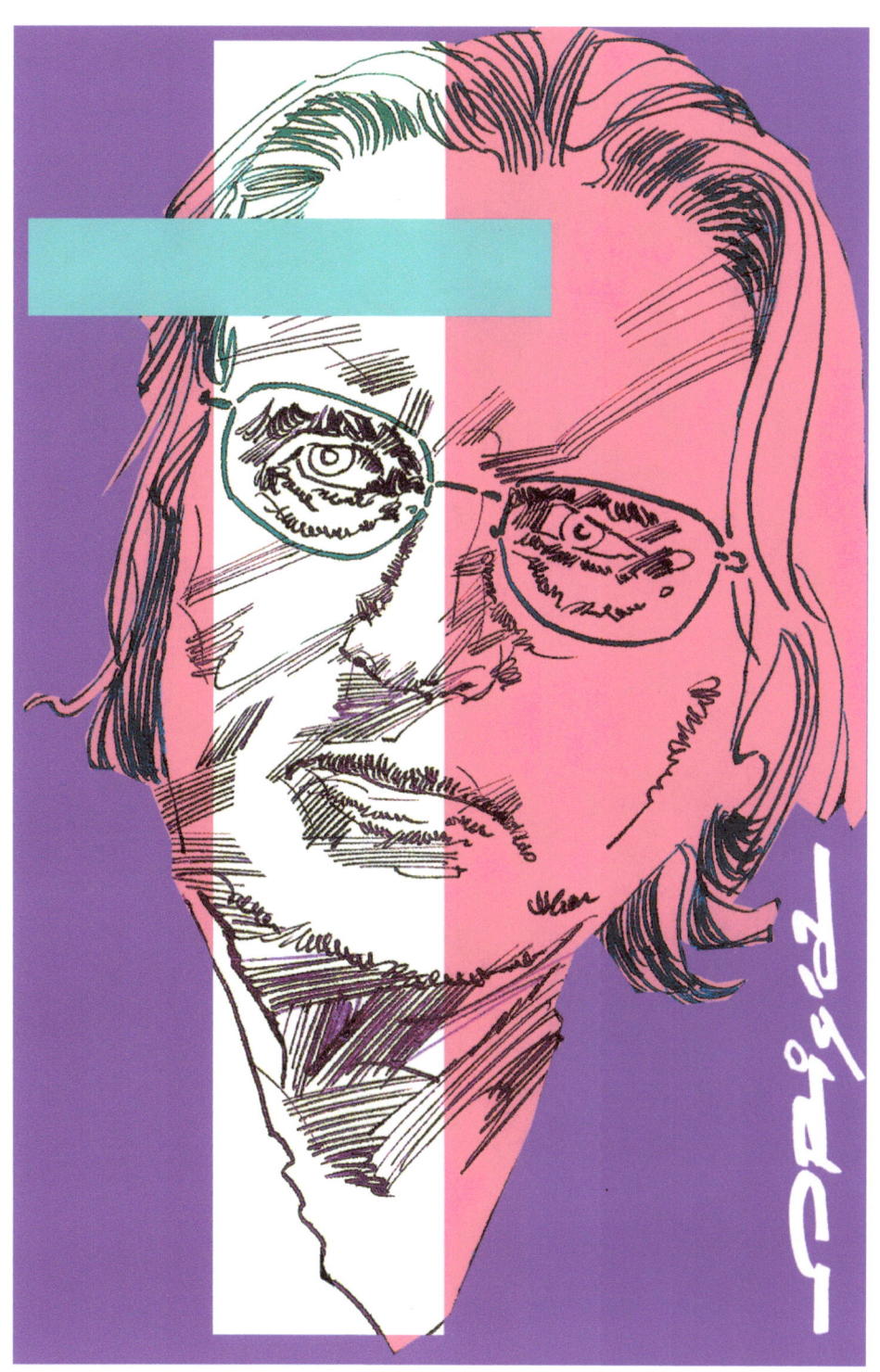

(41) Bruce Sterling

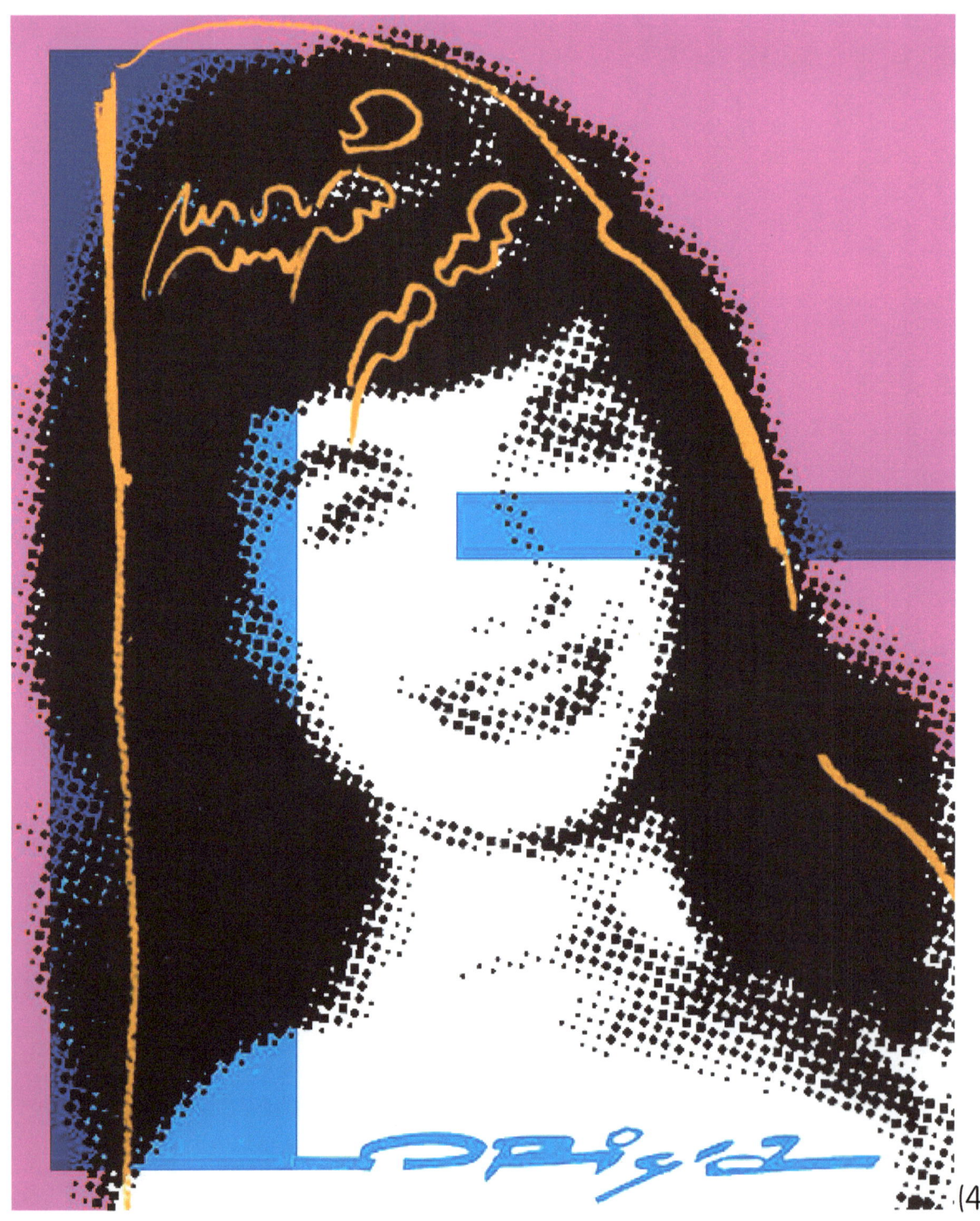

(42) Bettie Page

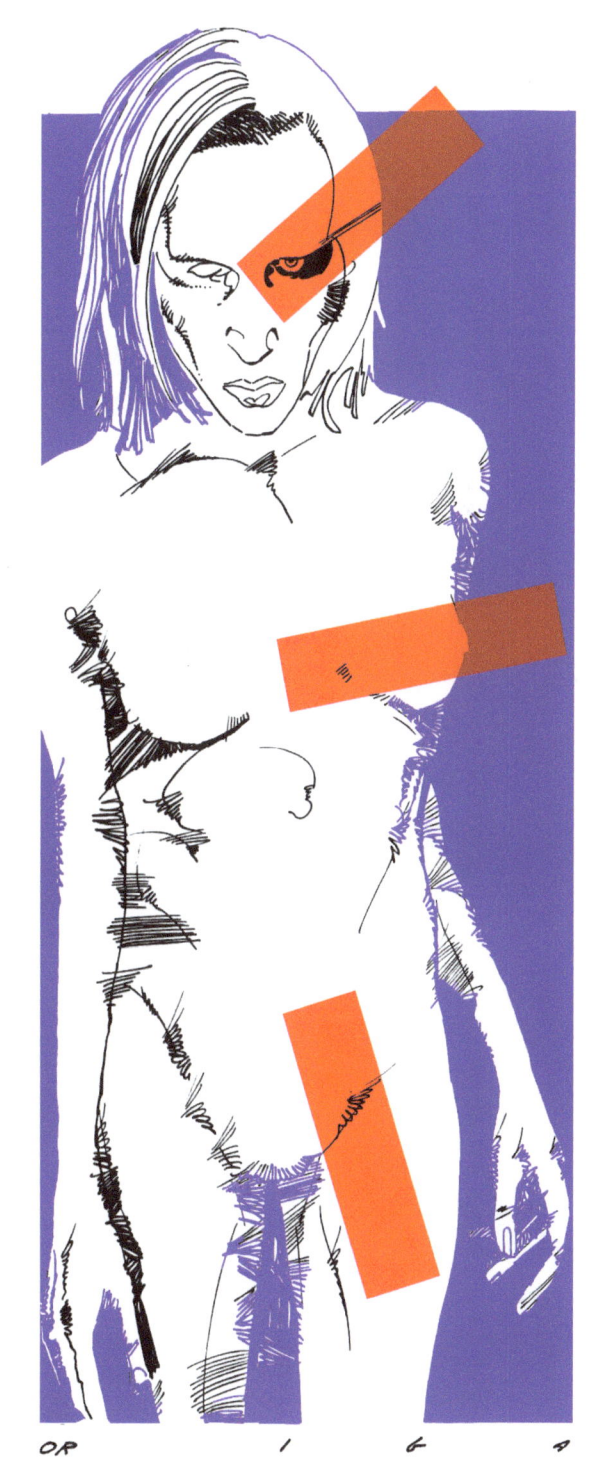

(43) Marilyn Manson

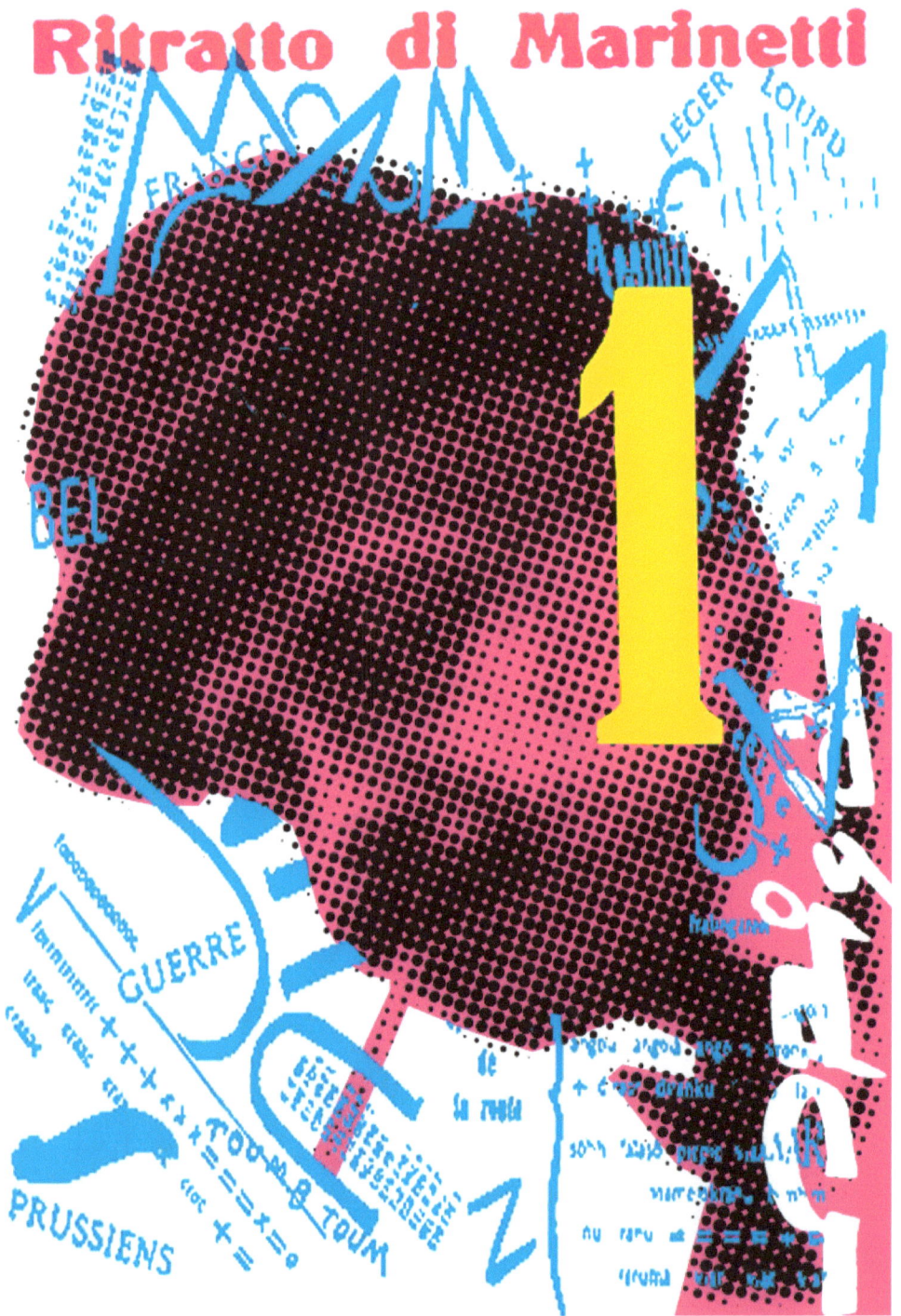

(44) Filippo Tommaso Marinetti

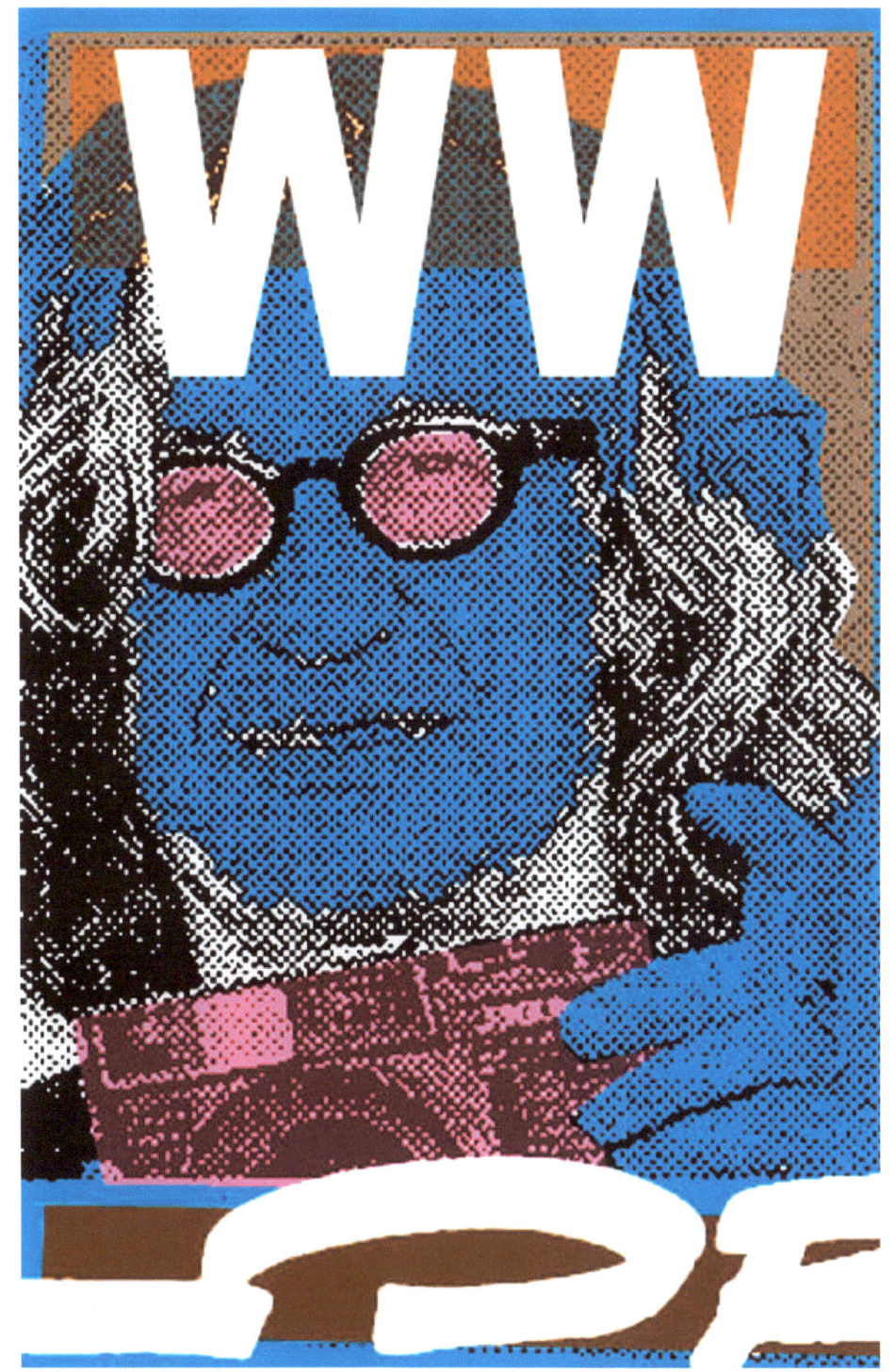

(45) Wim Wenders

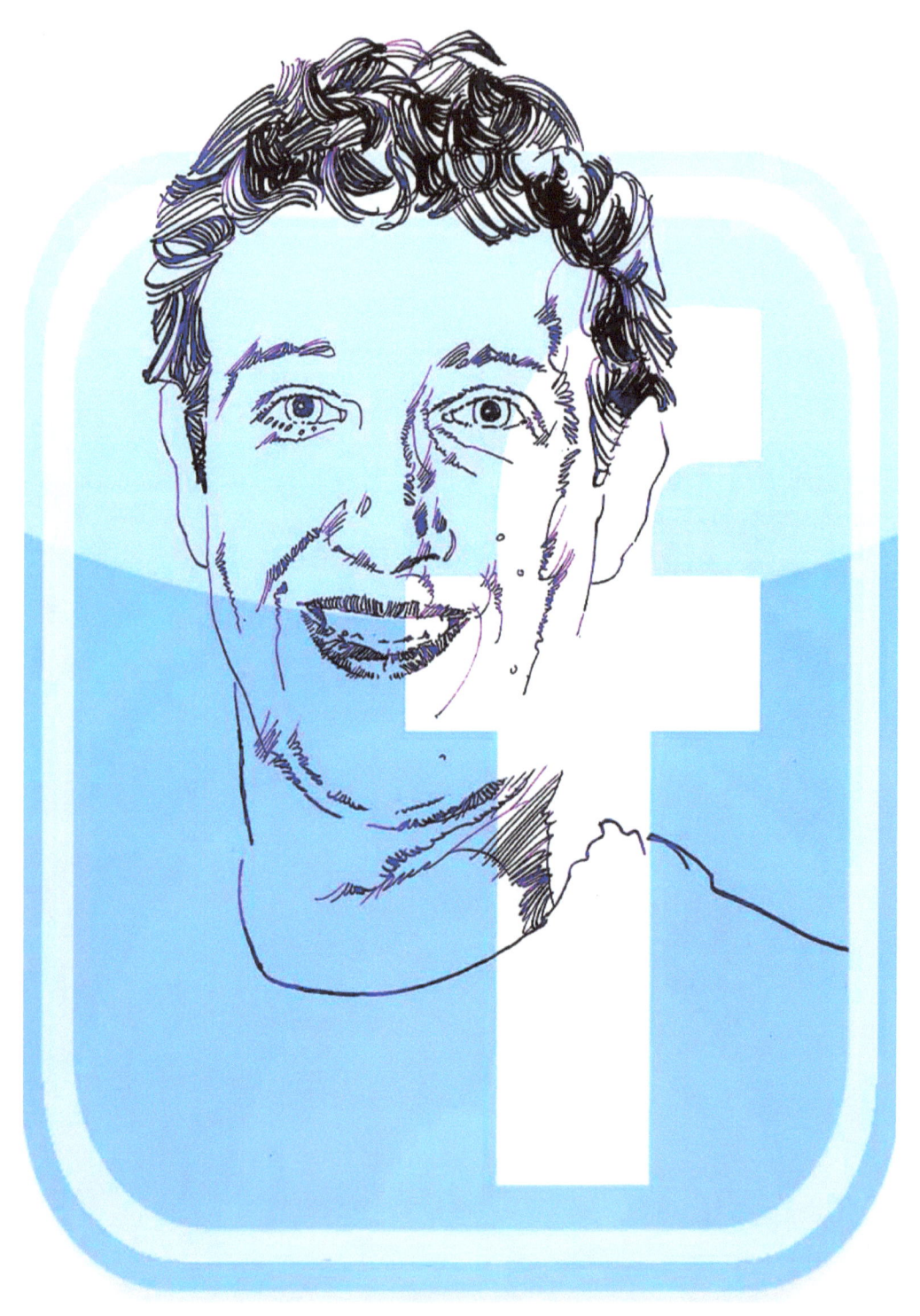

(46) Mark Zuckerberg

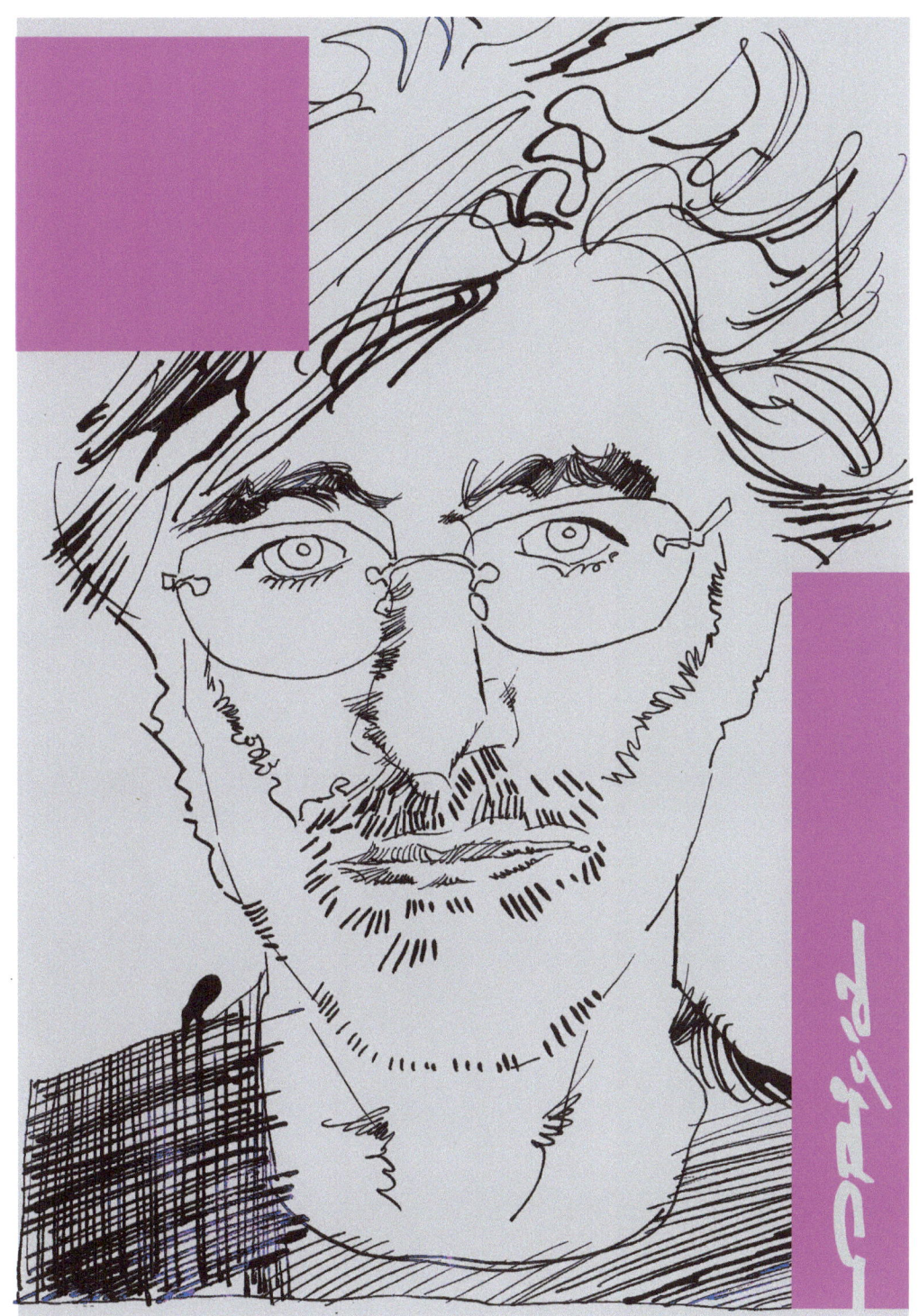

(47) Luca De Biase

www.ingramcontent.com/pod-product-compliance
Lightning Source LLC
Chambersburg PA
CBHW051059180526
45172CB00002B/708